INVENTIONS AND DISCOVERY

Jonas Salk and the Polio Vaccine

by Katherine Krohn

illustrated by Al Milgrom

Consultant:
David Oshinsky, PhD
Author of *Polio: An American Story*
Department of History
University of Texas at Austin
Austin, Texas

Capstone press®
Mankato, Minnesota

Graphic Library is published by Capstone Press,
1710 Roe Crest Drive, North Mankato, Minnesota 56003.
www.capstonepub.com

Library of Congress Cataloging-in-Publication Data
Krohn, Katherine E.
Jonas Salk and the polio vaccine / by Katherine Krohn ; illustrated by Al Milgrom.
p. cm.—(Graphic library. Inventions and discovery)
Summary: "In graphic novel format, tells the story of Jonas Salk's involvement in the development of a polio vaccine"—Provided by publisher.
Includes bibliographical references and index.
ISBN-13: 978-0-7368-6483-1 (hardcover) ISBN-10: 0-7368-6483-0 (hardcover)
ISBN-13: 978-0-7368-9645-0 (softcover pbk.) ISBN-10: 0-7368-9645-7 (softcover pbk.)
1. Salk, Jonas, 1914–1995. 2. Virologists—United States—Biography—Juvenile literature. 3. Poliomyelitis vaccine—Juvenile literature. I. Milgrom, A. (Allen), ill. II. Title. III. Series.
QR31.S25K76 2007
614.5'49092—dc22 2006008188

Designers
Jason Knudson and Juliette Peters

Colorist
Ken Steacy

Editor
Christopher Harbo

Editor's note: Direct quotations from primary sources are indicated by a yellow background.

Direct quotations appear on the following pages:
Page 16, from Dr. Thomas Francis' speech at the University of Michigan on April 12, 1955, as quoted in Jeffrey Kluger's *Splendid Solution: Jonas Salk and the Conquest of Polio* (New York: G. P. Putnam's Sons, 2004).
Page 18, from Dr. Jonas Salk's interview on the television program *See It Now* on April 12, 1955, as quoted in Richard Carter's *Breakthrough: The Saga of Jonas Salk* (New York: Trident Press, 1966).

Printed in the United States 5935

Table of Contents

Chapter 1
Respected Scientist

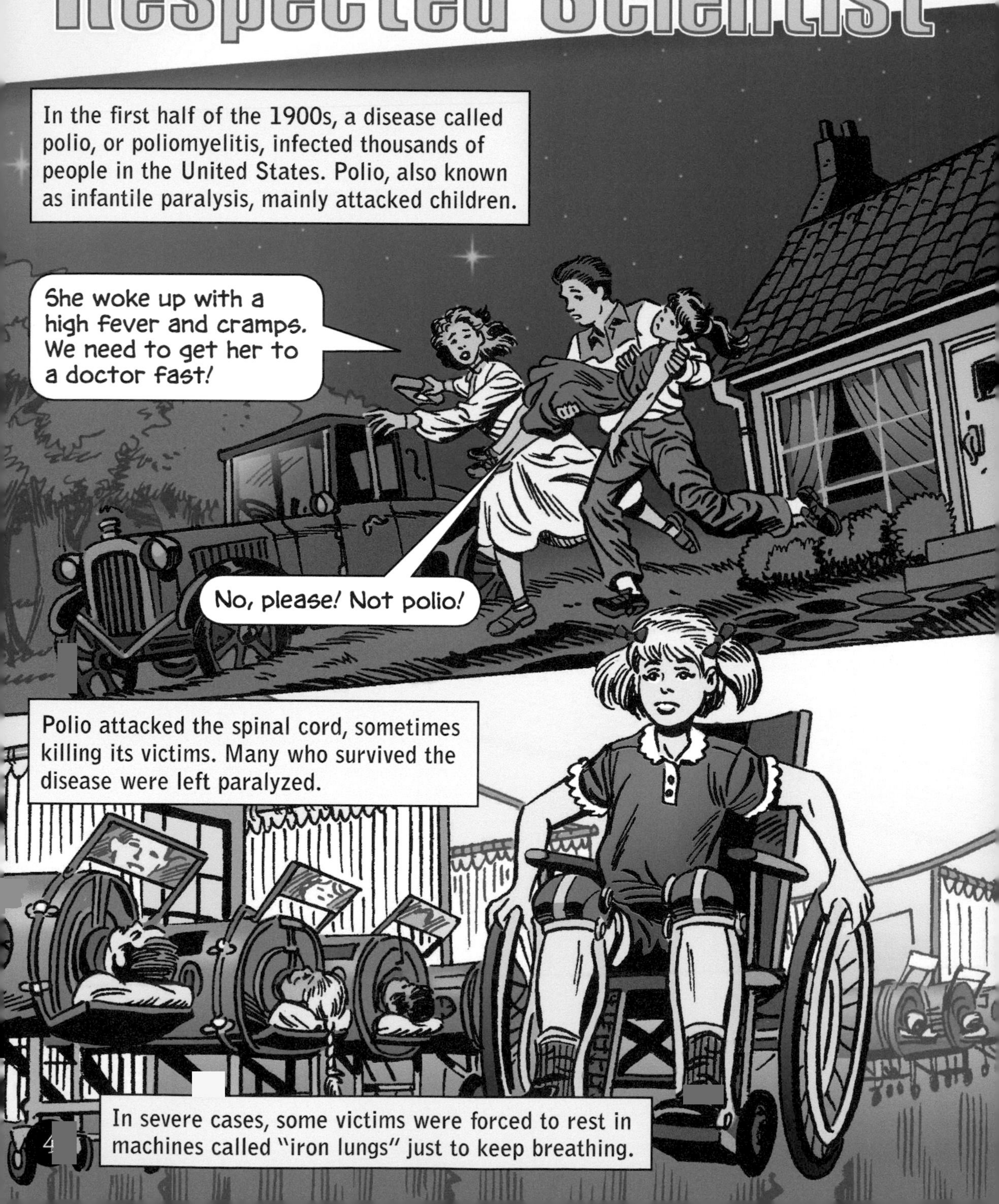

In the first half of the 1900s, a disease called polio, or poliomyelitis, infected thousands of people in the United States. Polio, also known as infantile paralysis, mainly attacked children.
She woke up with a high fever and cramps. We need to get her to a doctor fast!
No, please! Not polio!
Polio attacked the spinal cord, sometimes killing its victims. Many who survived the disease were left paralyzed.
In severe cases, some victims were forced to rest in machines called "iron lungs" just to keep breathing.

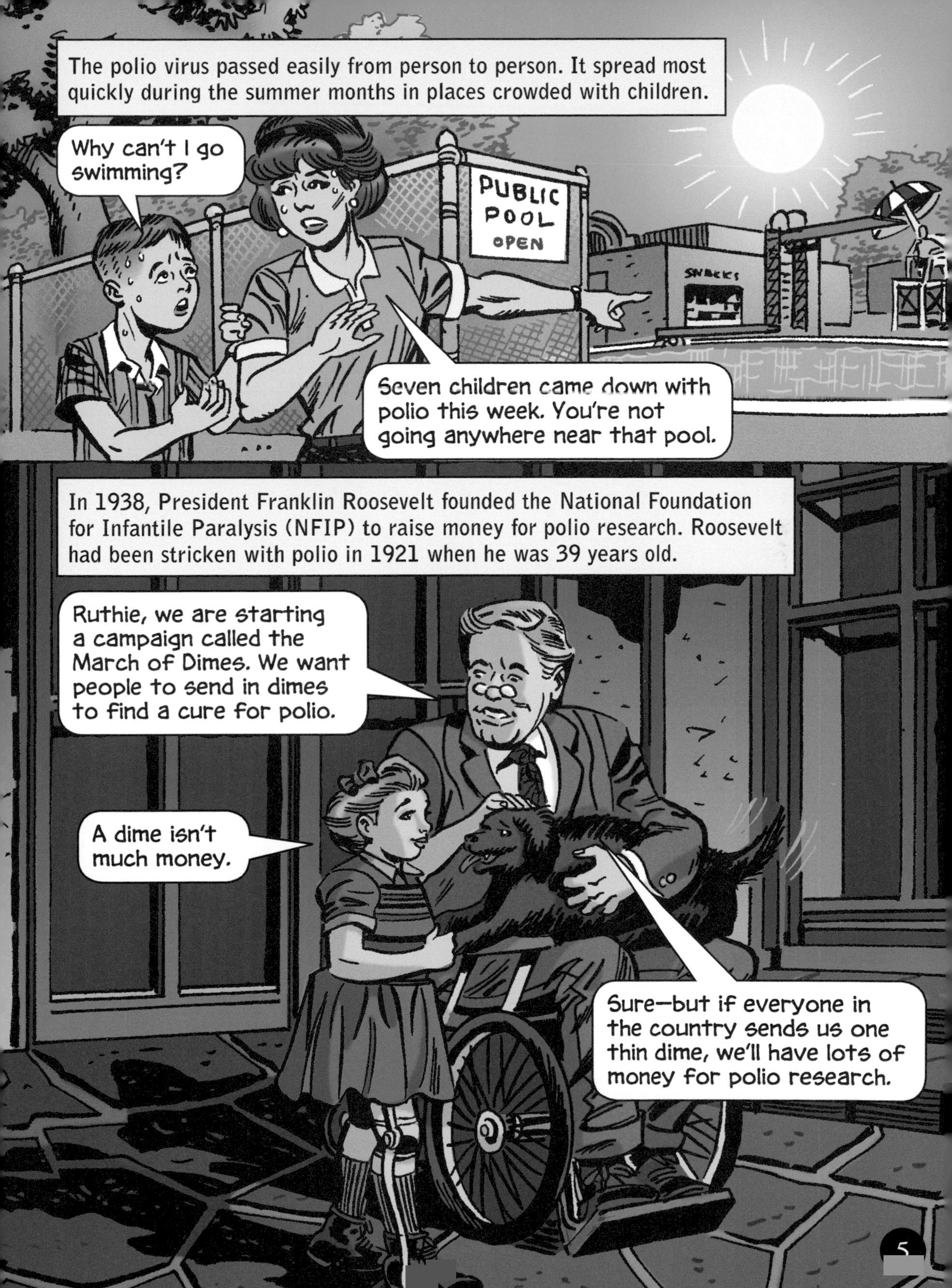
The polio virus passed easily from person to person. It spread most quickly during the summer months in places crowded with children.
Why can't I go swimming?
PUBLIC POOL OPEN
Seven children came down with polio this week. You're not going anywhere near that pool.
In 1938, President Franklin Roosevelt founded the National Foundation for Infantile Paralysis (NFIP) to raise money for polio research. Roosevelt had been stricken with polio in 1921 when he was 39 years old.
Ruthie, we are starting a campaign called the March of Dimes. We want people to send in dimes to find a cure for polio.
A dime isn't much money.
Sure—but if everyone in the country sends us one thin dime, we'll have lots of money for polio research.

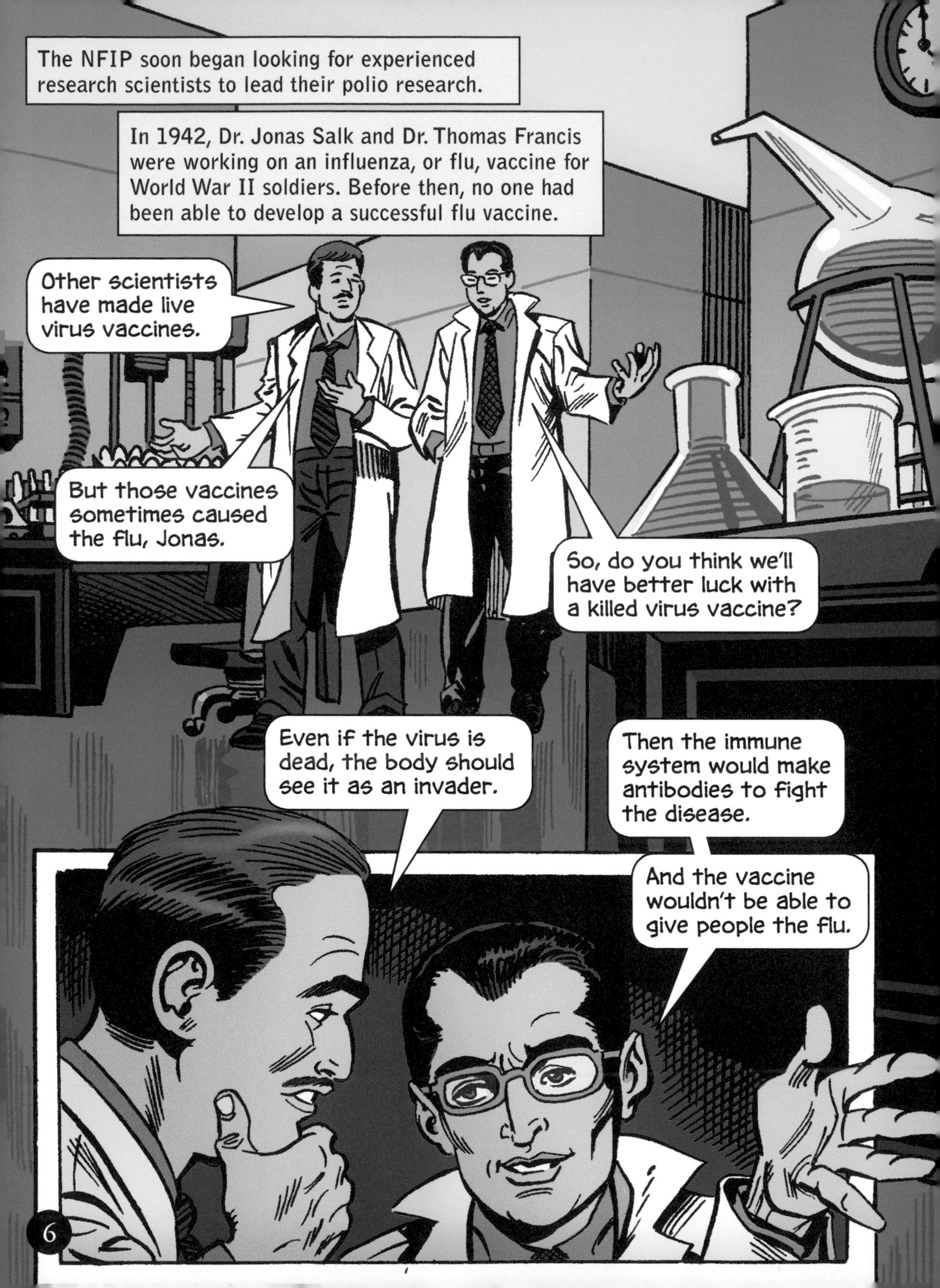
The NFIP soon began looking for experienced research scientists to lead their polio research.
In 1942, Dr. Jonas Salk and Dr. Thomas Francis were working on an influenza, or flu, vaccine for World War II soldiers. Before then, no one had been able to develop a successful flu vaccine.
Other scientists have made live virus vaccines.
But those vaccines sometimes caused the flu, Jonas.
So, do you think we'll have better luck with a killed virus vaccine?
Even if the virus is dead, the body should see it as an invader.
Then the immune system would make antibodies to fight the disease.
And the vaccine wouldn't be able to give people the flu.

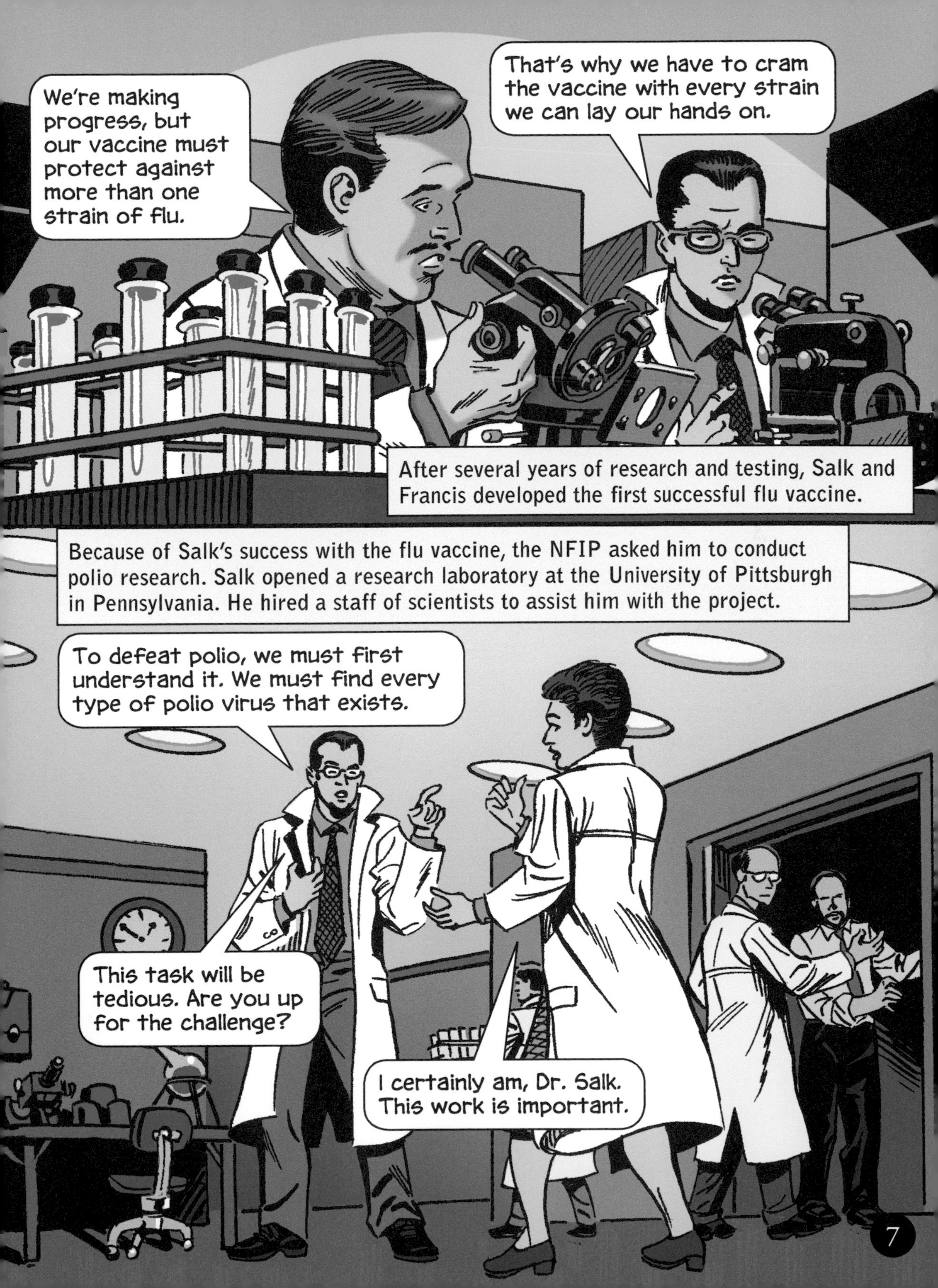
We're making progress, but our vaccine must protect against more than one strain of flu.
That's why we have to cram the vaccine with every strain we can lay our hands on.
After several years of research and testing, Salk and Francis developed the first successful flu vaccine.
Because of Salk's success with the flu vaccine, the NFIP asked him to conduct polio research. Salk opened a research laboratory at the University of Pittsburgh in Pennsylvania. He hired a staff of scientists to assist him with the project.
To defeat polio, we must first understand it. We must find every type of polio virus that exists.
This task will be tedious. Are you up for the challenge?
I certainly am, Dr. Salk. This work is important.

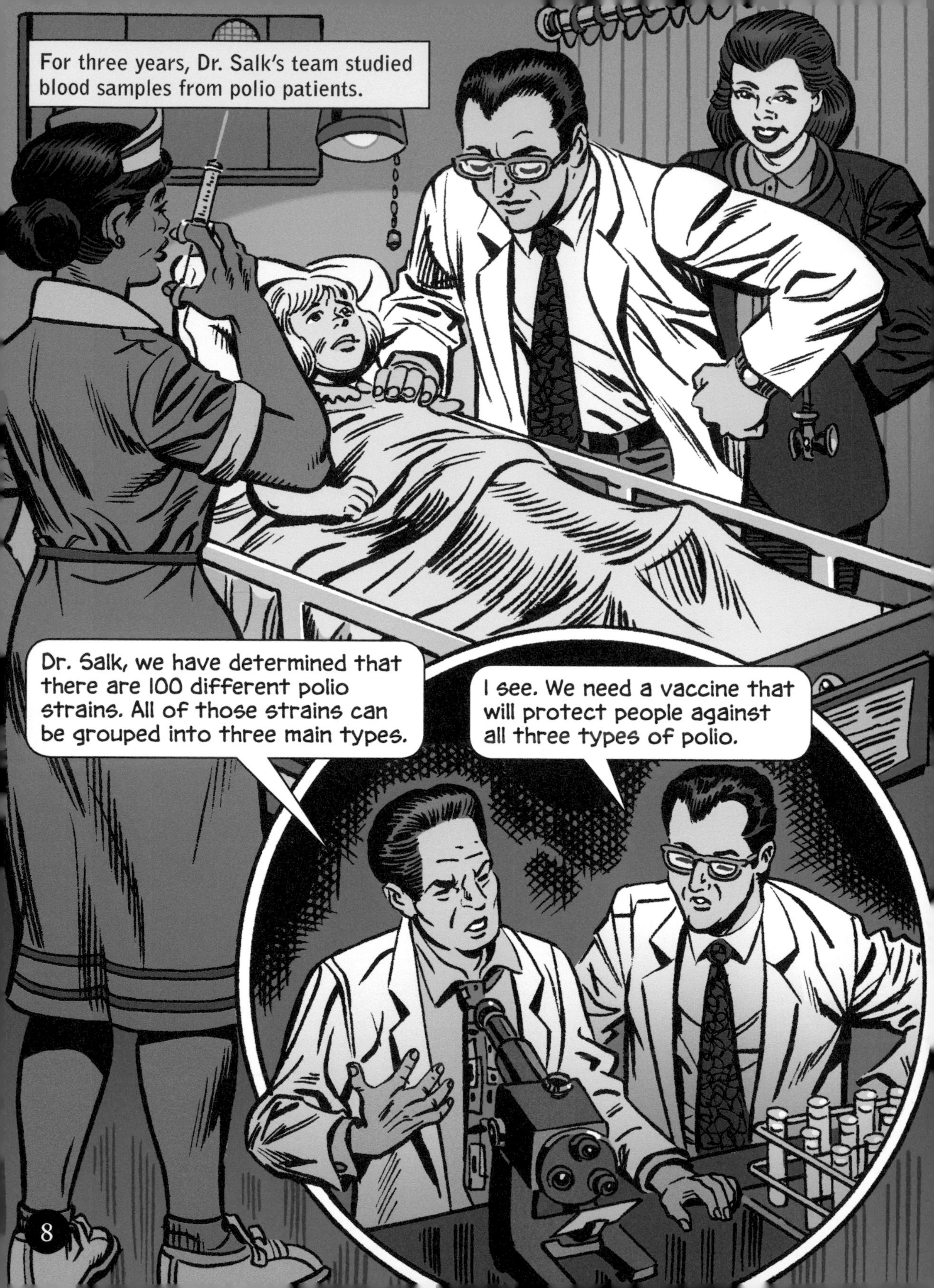
For three years, Dr. Salk's team studied blood samples from polio patients.
Dr. Salk, we have determined that there are 100 different polio strains. All of those strains can be grouped into three main types.
I see. We need a vaccine that will protect people against all three types of polio.

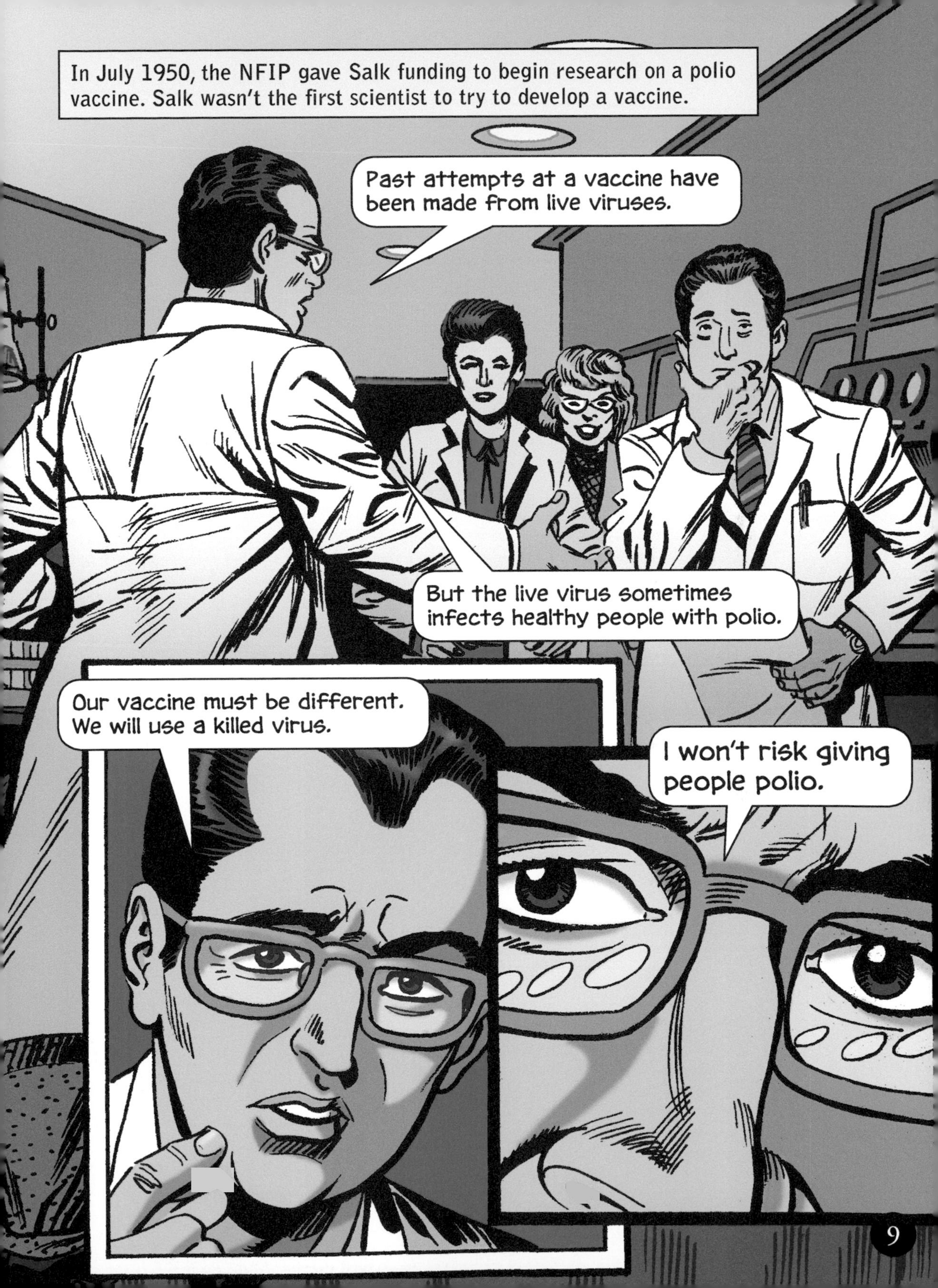
In July 1950, the NFIP gave Salk funding to begin research on a polio vaccine. Salk wasn't the first scientist to try to develop a vaccine.
Past attempts at a vaccine have been made from live viruses.
But the live virus sometimes infects healthy people with polio.
Our vaccine must be different. We will use a killed virus.
I won't risk giving people polio.

Chapter 2
Important Research

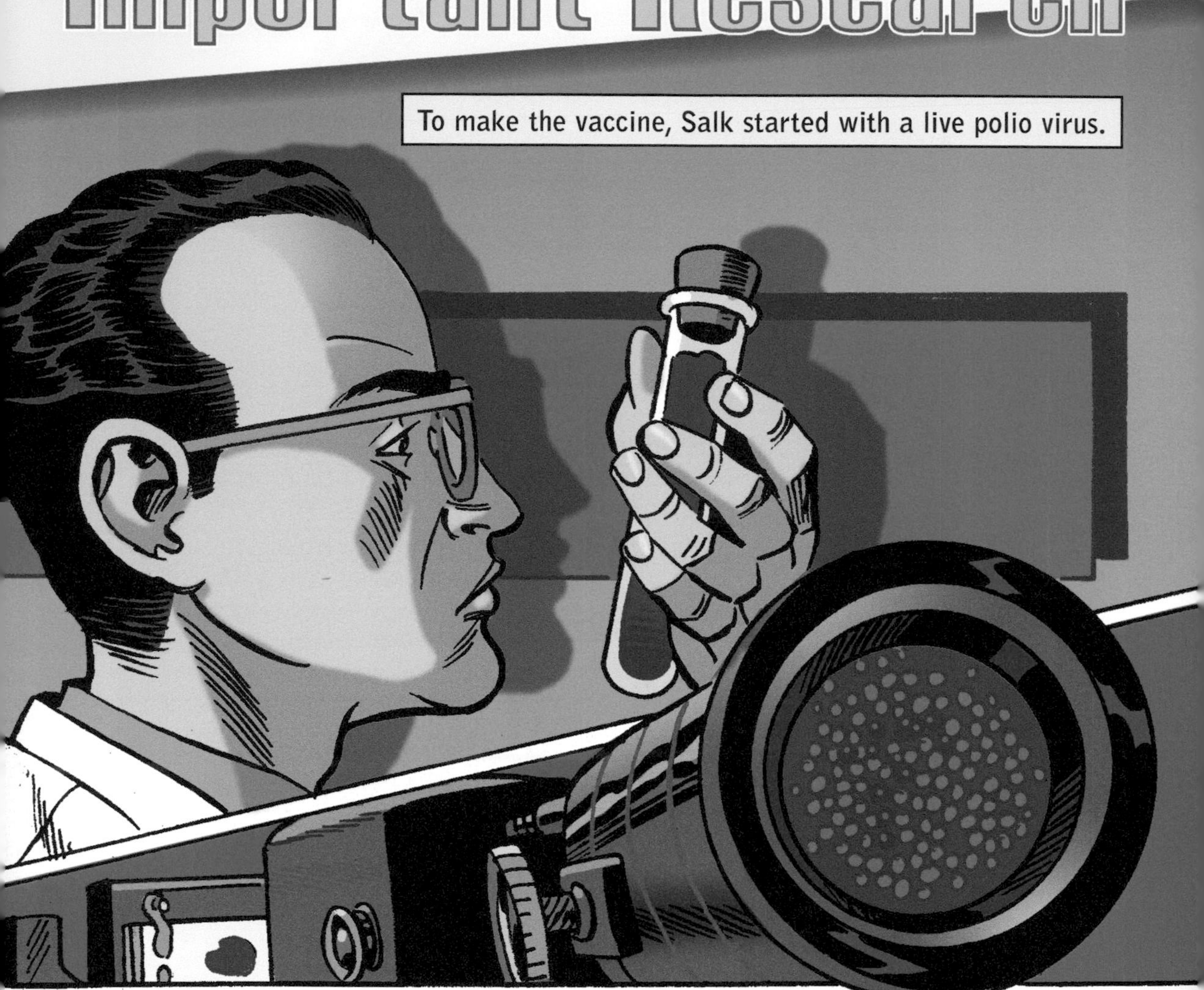
To make the vaccine, Salk started with a live polio virus.

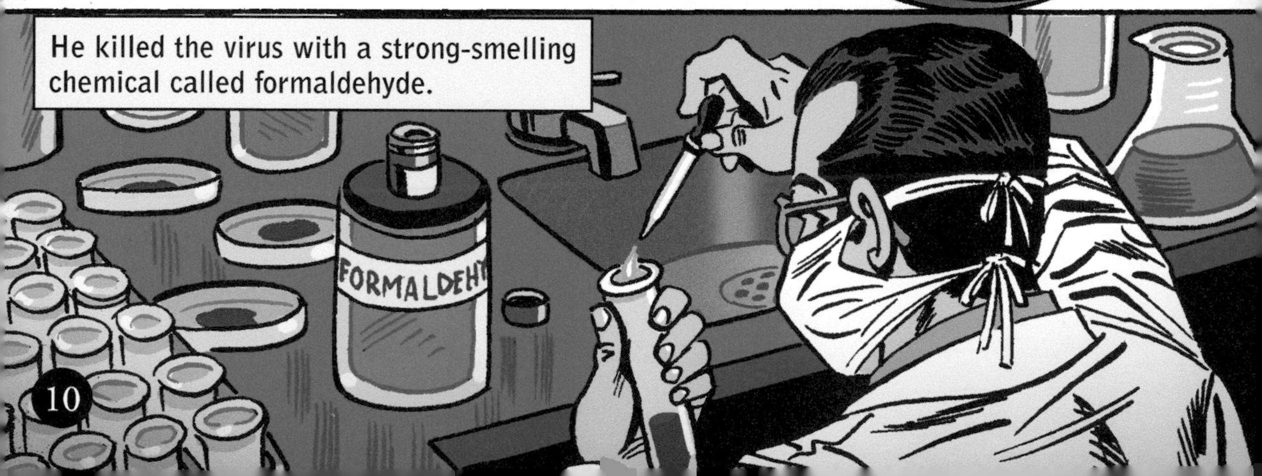
He killed the virus with a strong-smelling chemical called formaldehyde.
FORMALDEHY

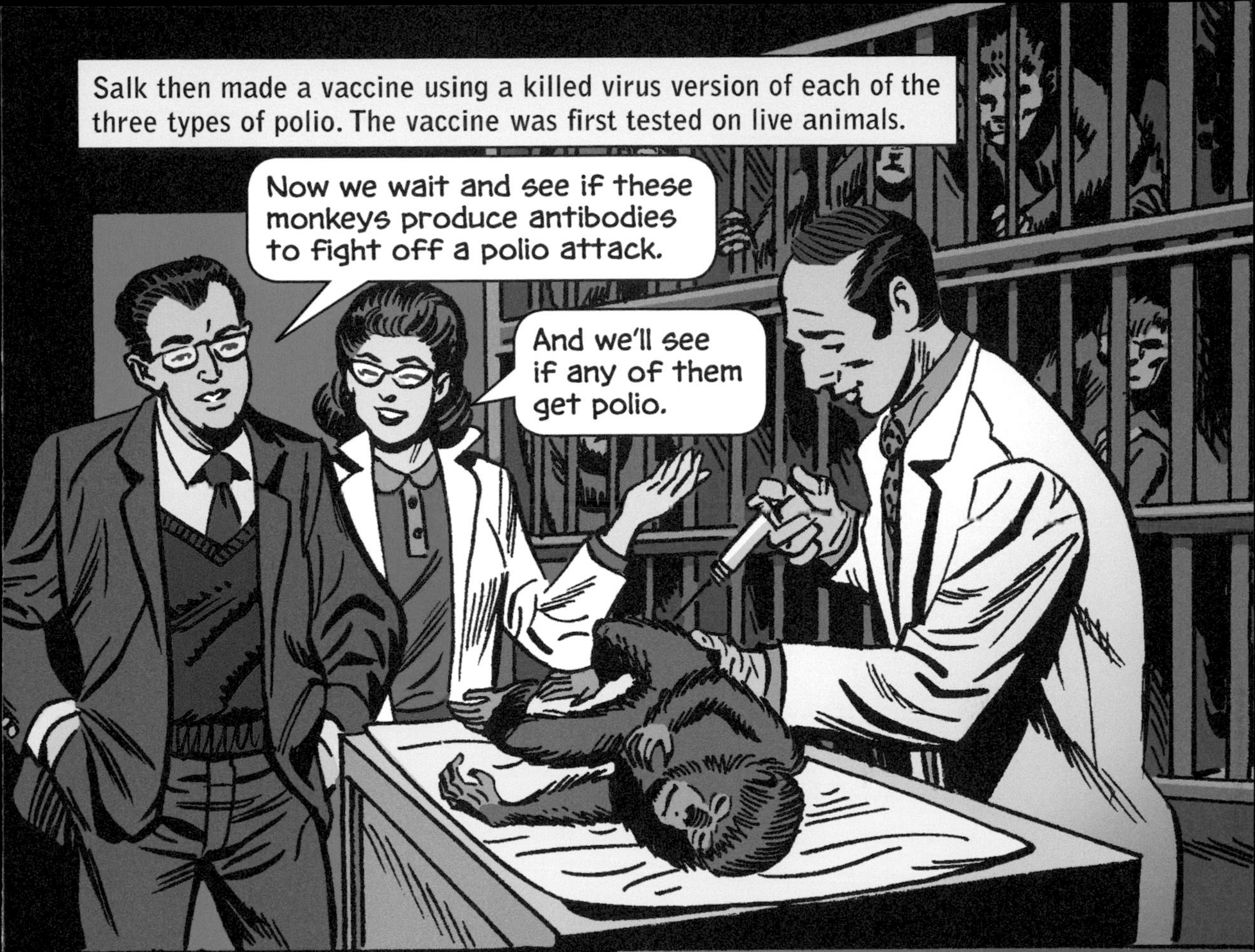
Salk then made a vaccine using a killed virus version of each of the three types of polio. The vaccine was first tested on live animals.
Now we wait and see if these monkeys produce antibodies to fight off a polio attack.
And we'll see if any of them get polio.

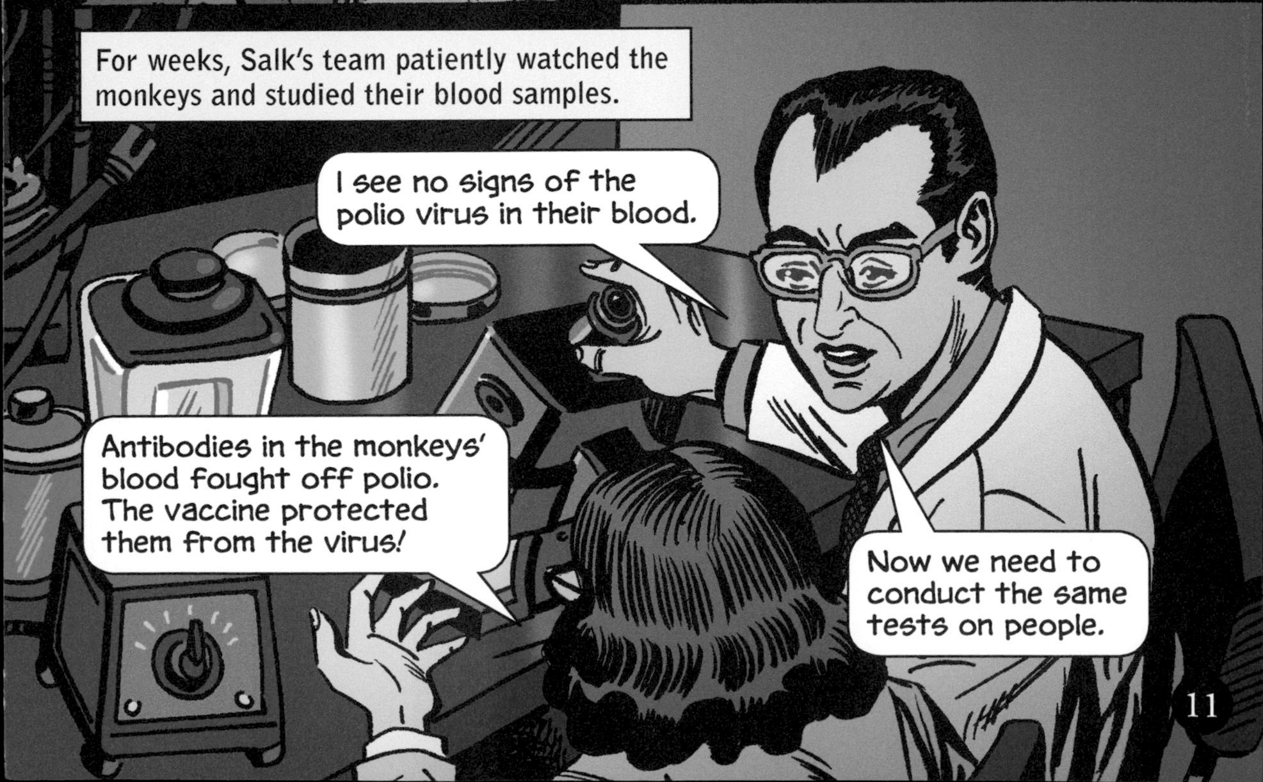
For weeks, Salk's team patiently watched the monkeys and studied their blood samples.
I see no signs of the polio virus in their blood.
Antibodies in the monkeys' blood fought off polio. The vaccine protected them from the virus!
Now we need to conduct the same tests on people.

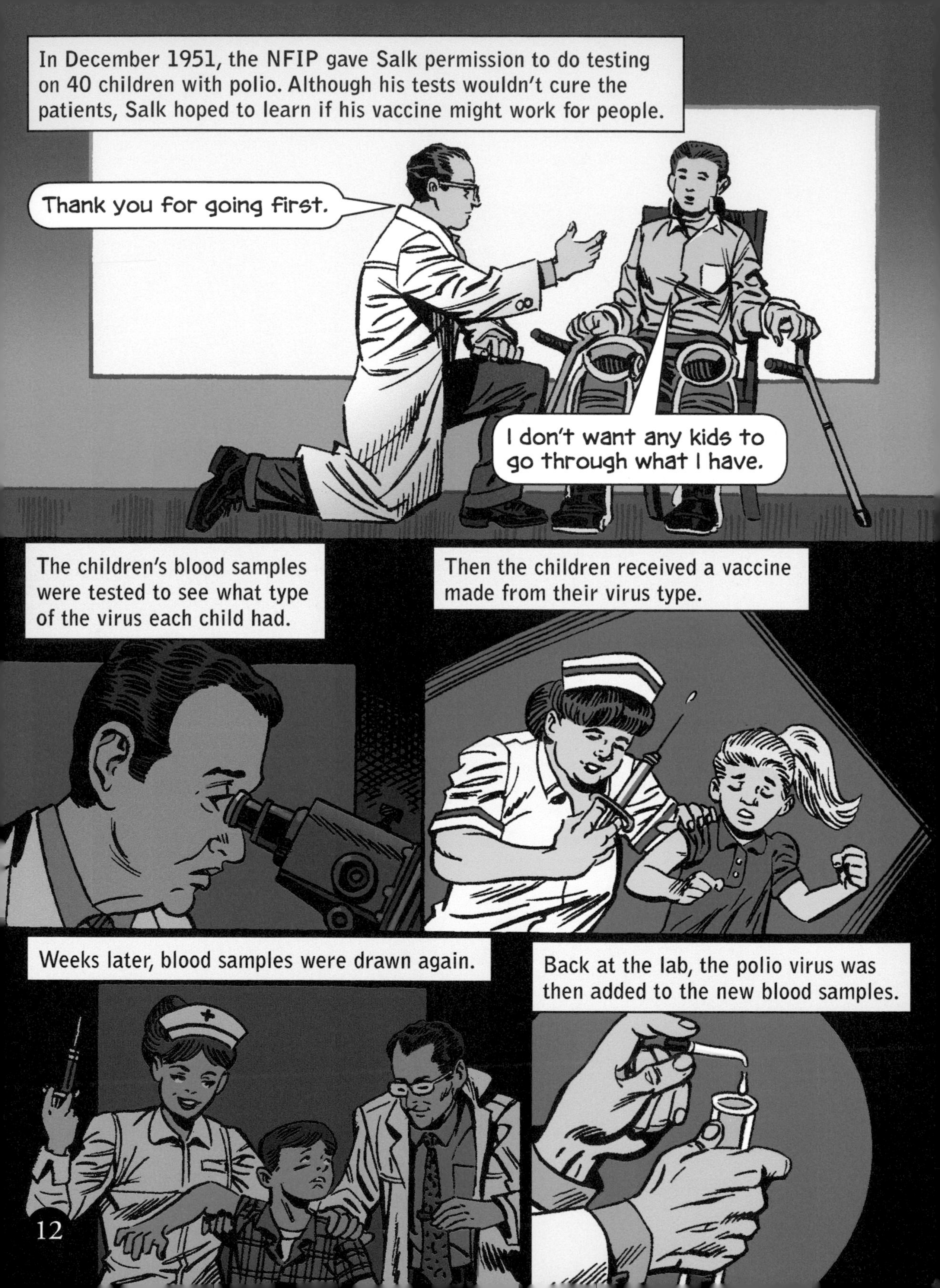
In December 1951, the NFIP gave Salk permission to do testing on 40 children with polio. Although his tests wouldn't cure the patients, Salk hoped to learn if his vaccine might work for people.
Thank you for going first.
I don't want any kids to go through what I have.
The children's blood samples were tested to see what type of the virus each child had.
Then the children received a vaccine made from their virus type.
Weeks later, blood samples were drawn again.
Back at the lab, the polio virus was then added to the new blood samples.

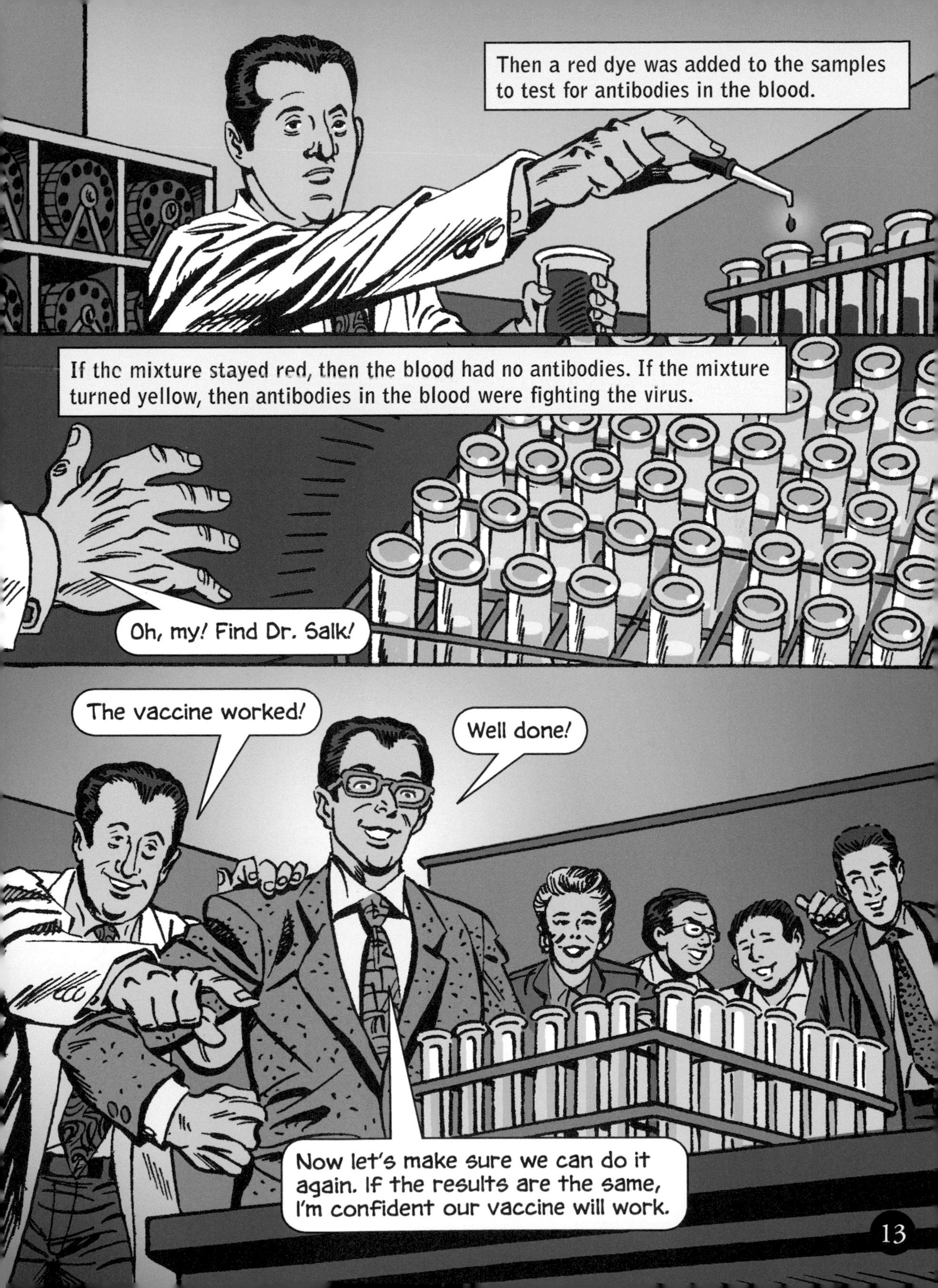
Then a red dye was added to the samples to test for antibodies in the blood.
If the mixture stayed red, then the blood had no antibodies. If the mixture turned yellow, then antibodies in the blood were fighting the virus.
Oh, my! Find Dr. Salk!
The vaccine worked!
Well done!
Now let's make sure we can do it again. If the results are the same, I'm confident our vaccine will work.

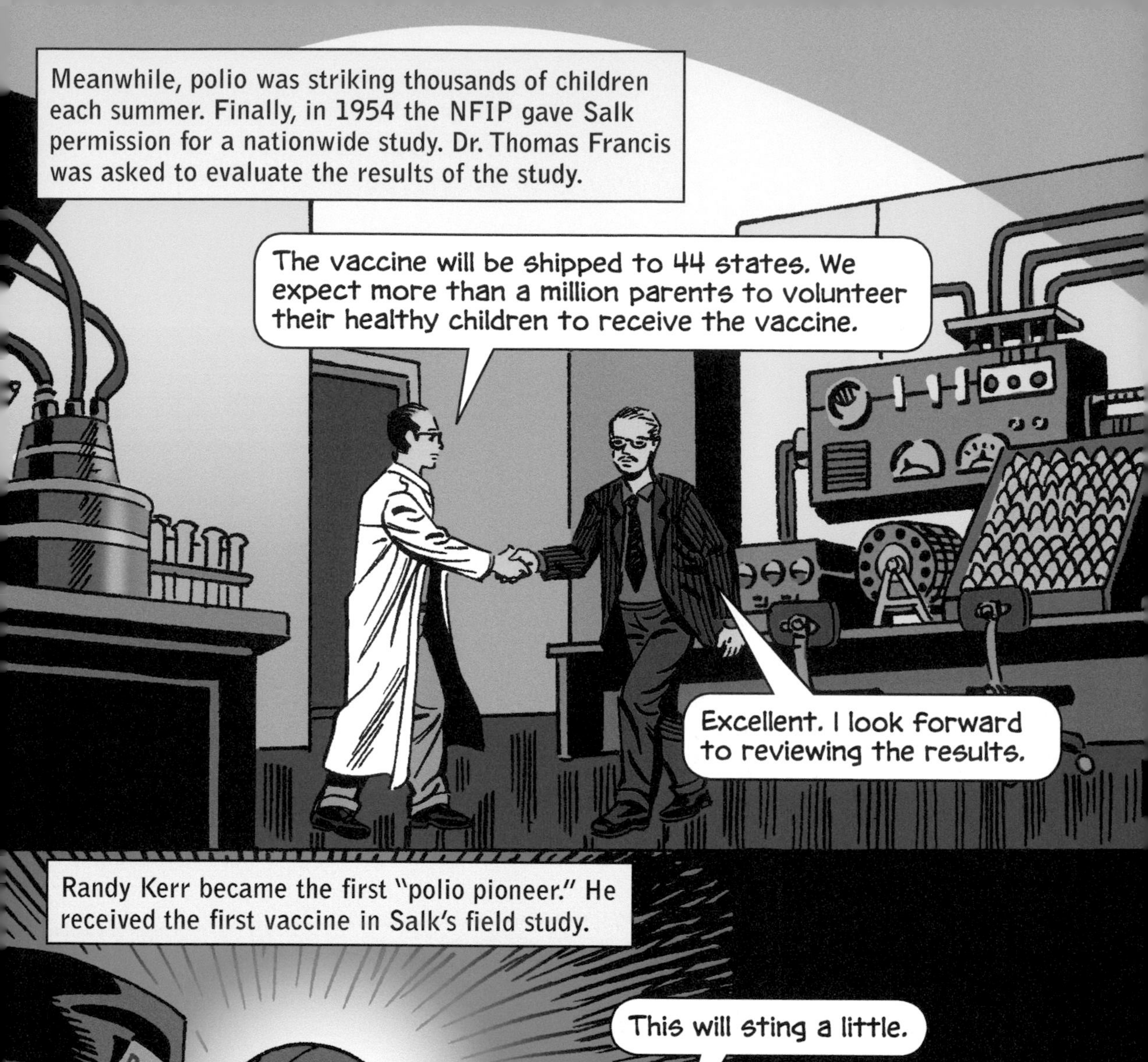
Meanwhile, polio was striking thousands of children each summer. Finally, in 1954 the NFIP gave Salk permission for a nationwide study. Dr. Thomas Francis was asked to evaluate the results of the study.
The vaccine will be shipped to 44 states. We expect more than a million parents to volunteer their healthy children to receive the vaccine.
Excellent. I look forward to reviewing the results.

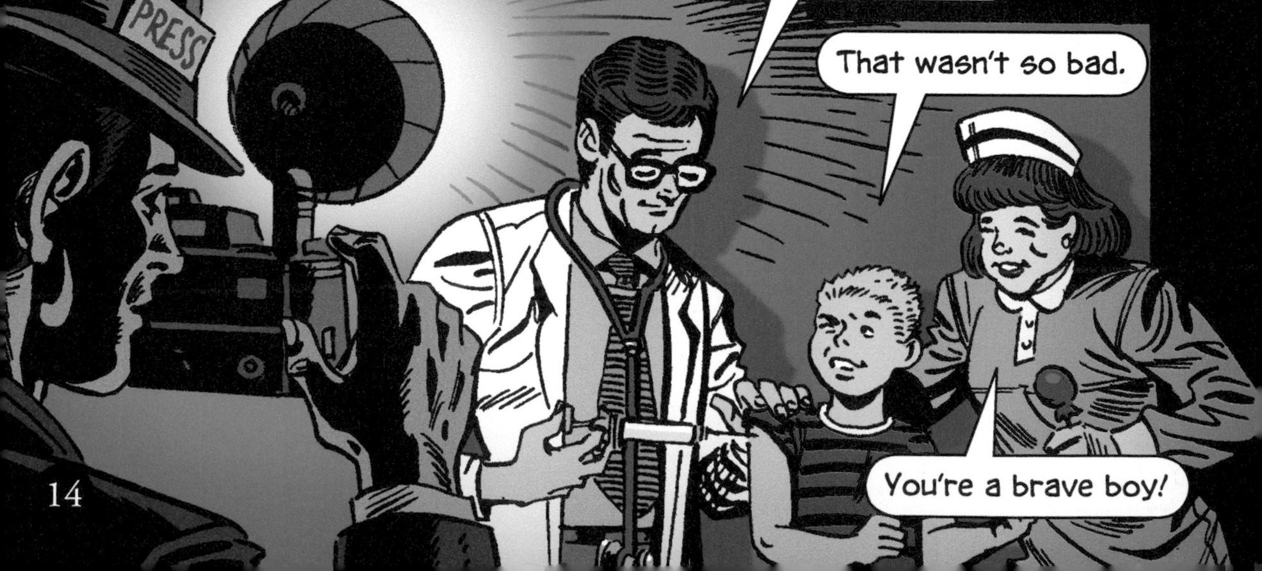
Randy Kerr became the first "polio pioneer." He received the first vaccine in Salk's field study.
PRESS
This will sting a little.
That wasn't so bad.
You're a brave boy!

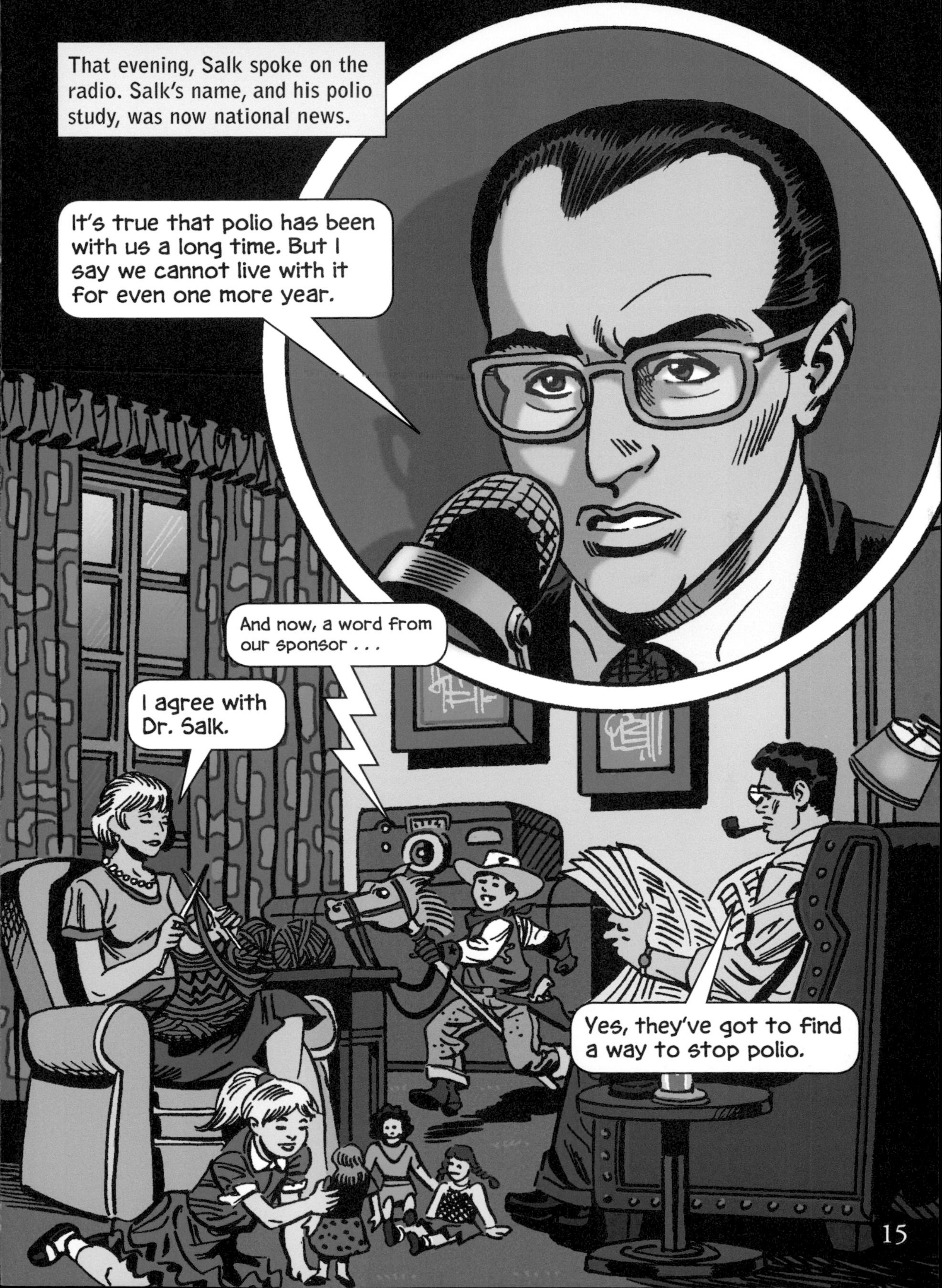
That evening, Salk spoke on the radio. Salk's name, and his polio study, was now national news.
It's true that polio has been with us a long time. But I say we cannot live with it for even one more year.
And now, a word from our sponsor . . .
I agree with Dr. Salk.
Yes, they've got to find a way to stop polio.

Chapter 3

National Hero

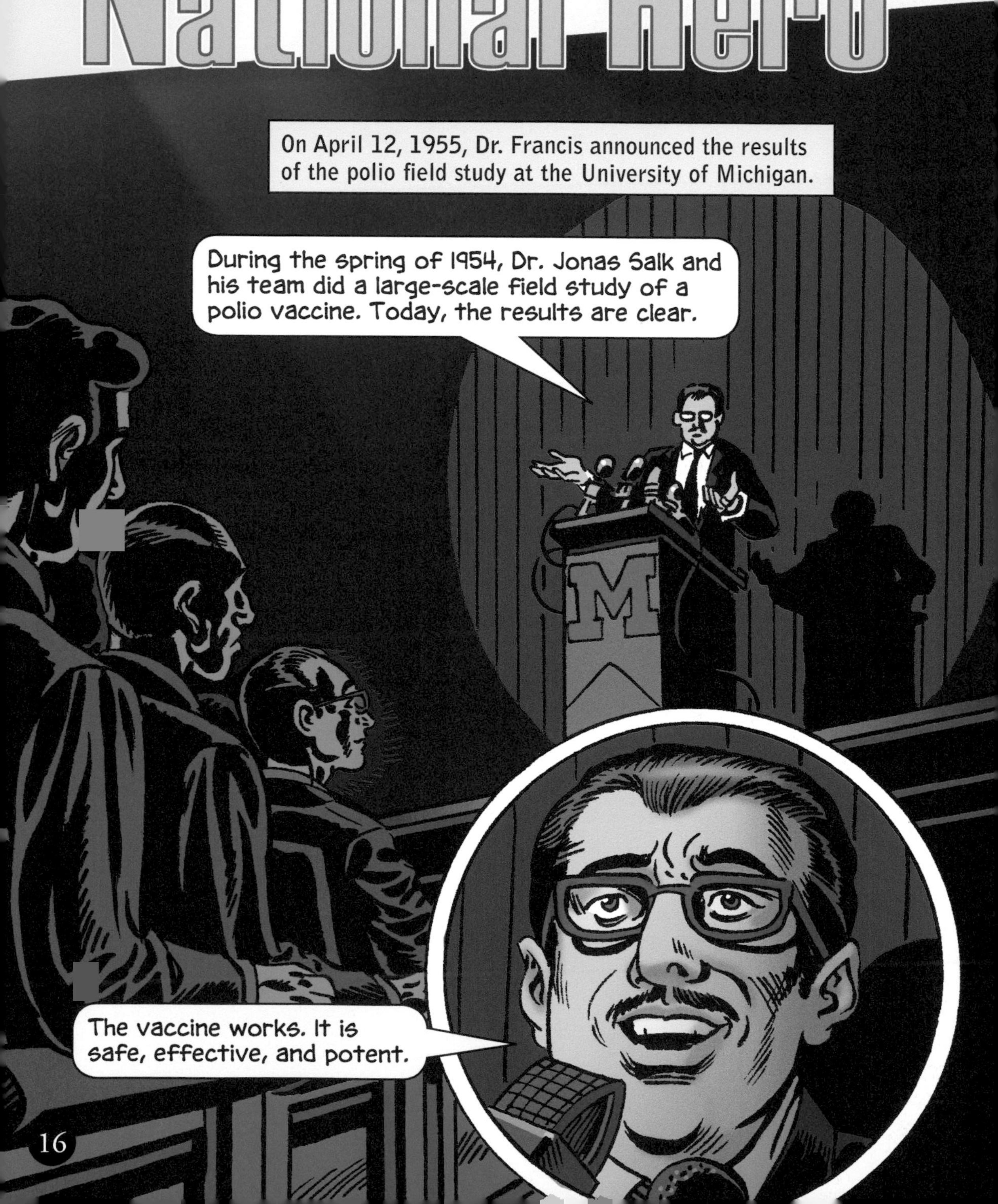
On April 12, 1955, Dr. Francis announced the results of the polio field study at the University of Michigan.
During the spring of 1954, Dr. Jonas Salk and his team did a large-scale field study of a polio vaccine. Today, the results are clear.
M
The vaccine works. It is safe, effective, and potent.

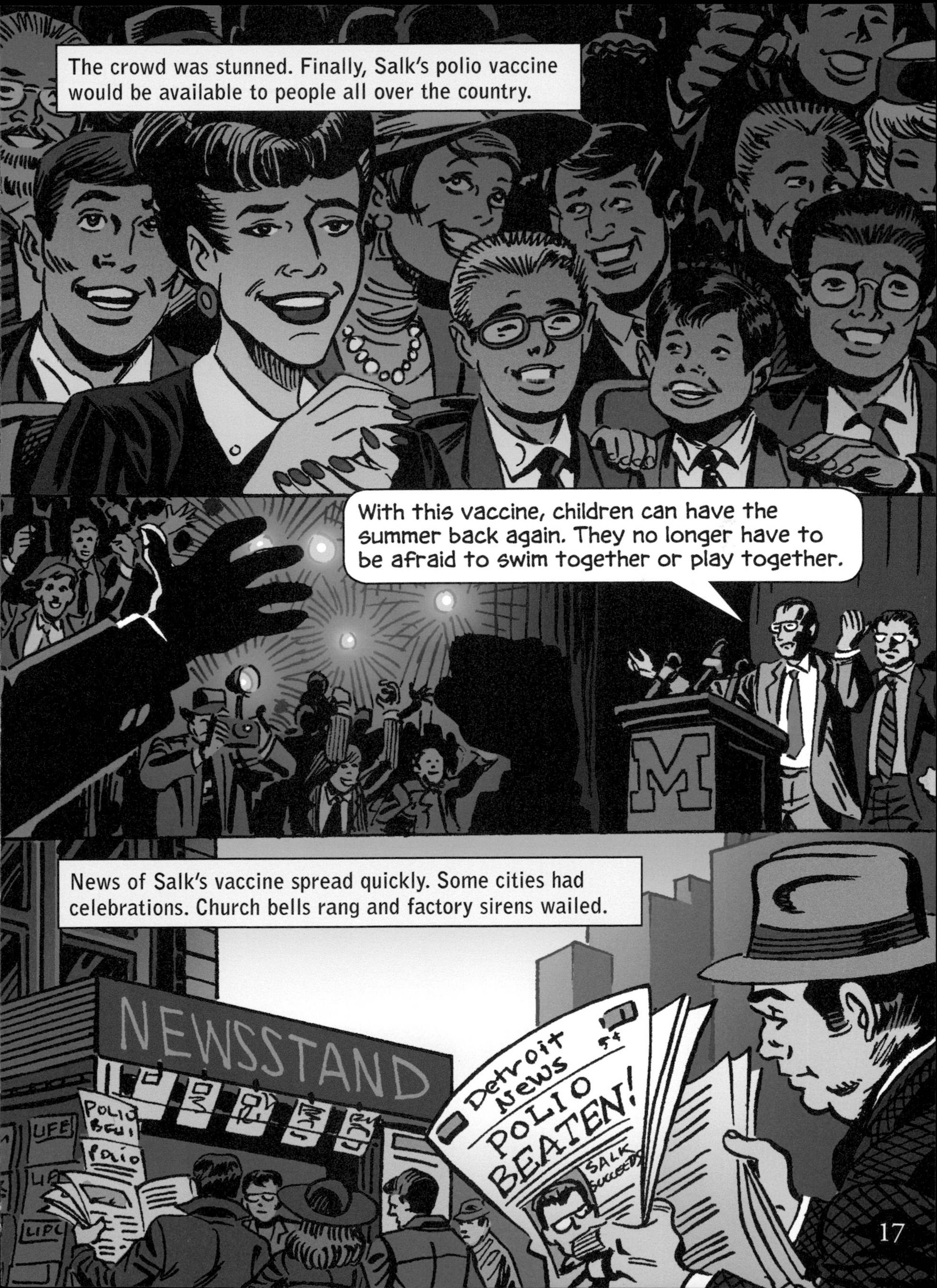

The crowd was stunned. Finally, Salk's polio vaccine would be available to people all over the country.
With this vaccine, children can have the summer back again. They no longer have to be afraid to swim together or play together.
M
News of Salk's vaccine spread quickly. Some cities had celebrations. Church bells rang and factory sirens wailed.
NEWSSTAND
Detroit News
5¢
POLIO BEATEN!
SALK

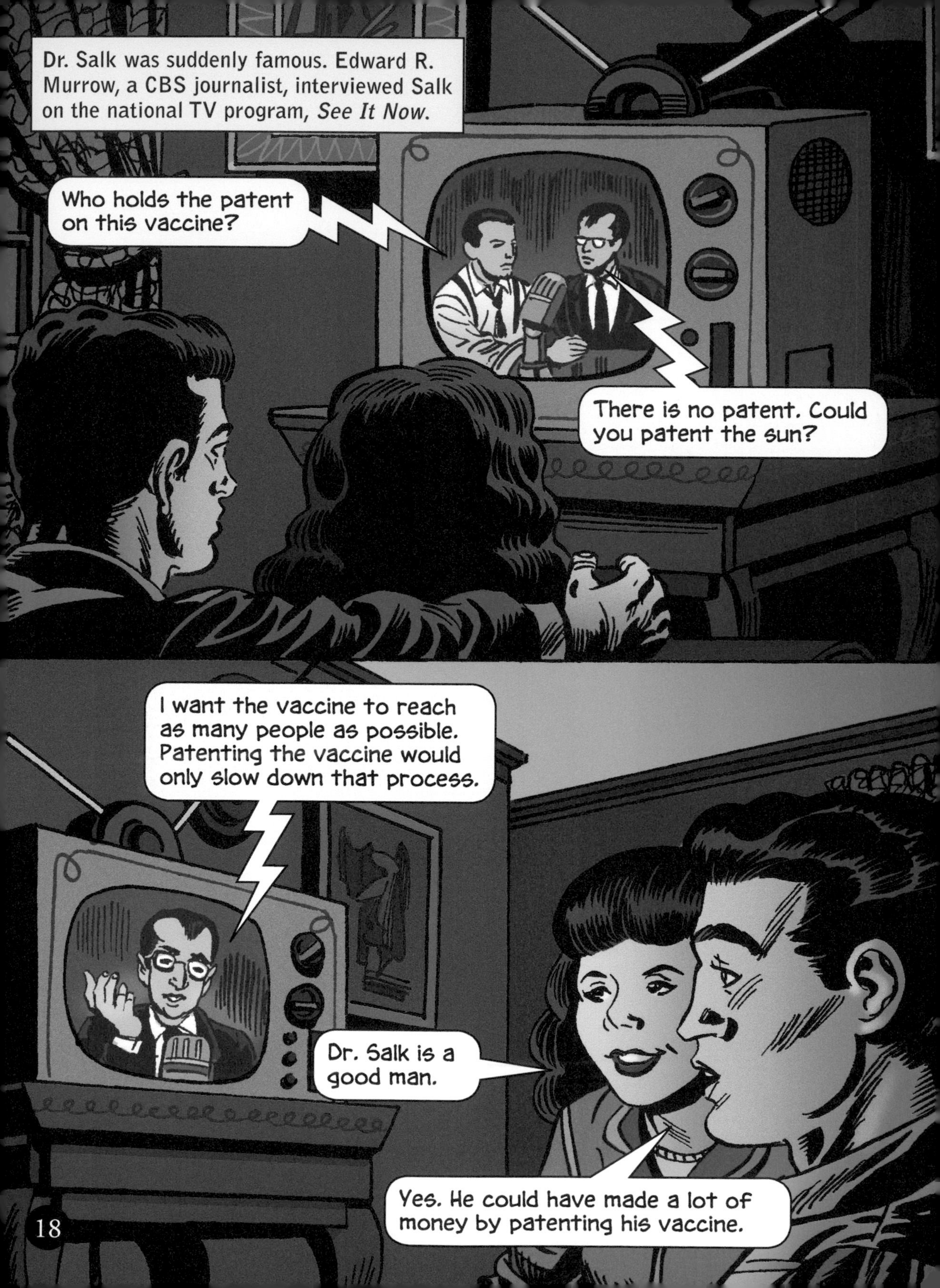
Dr. Salk was suddenly famous. Edward R. Murrow, a CBS journalist, interviewed Salk on the national TV program, *See It Now*.
Who holds the patent on this vaccine?
There is no patent. Could you patent the sun?
I want the vaccine to reach as many people as possible. Patenting the vaccine would only slow down that process.
Dr. Salk is a good man.
Yes. He could have made a lot of money by patenting his vaccine.

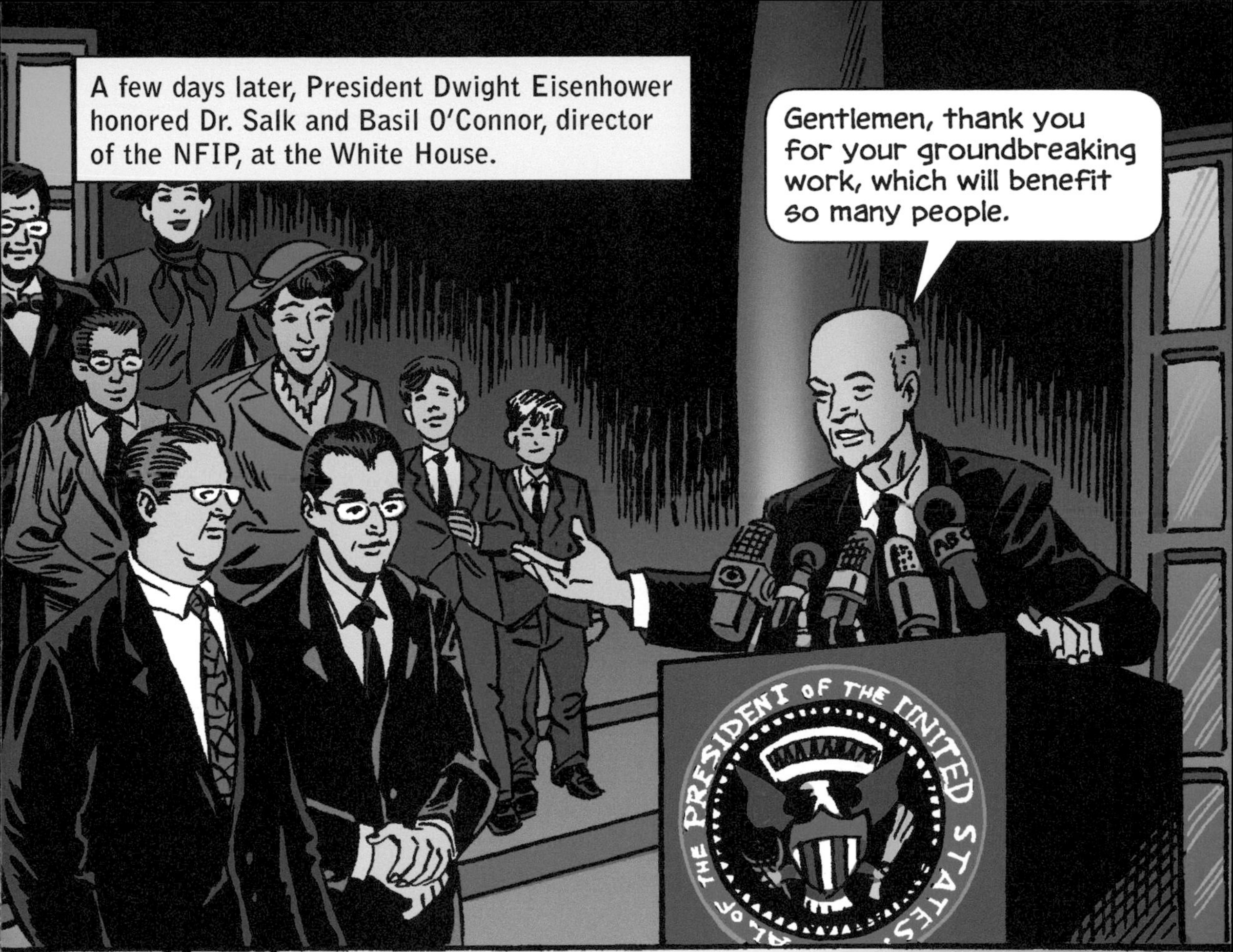
A few days later, President Dwight Eisenhower honored Dr. Salk and Basil O'Connor, director of the NFIP, at the White House.
Gentlemen, thank you for your groundbreaking work, which will benefit so many people.

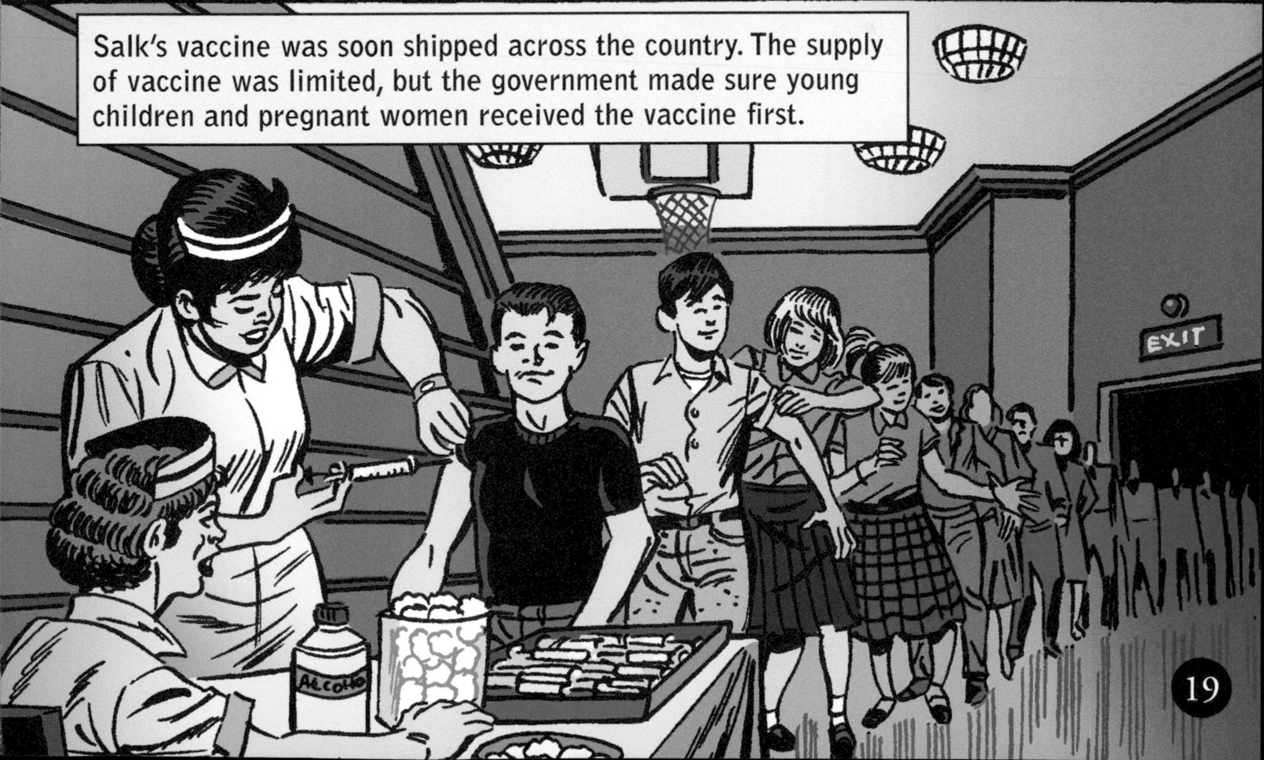
Salk's vaccine was soon shipped across the country. The supply of vaccine was limited, but the government made sure young children and pregnant women received the vaccine first.
EXIT

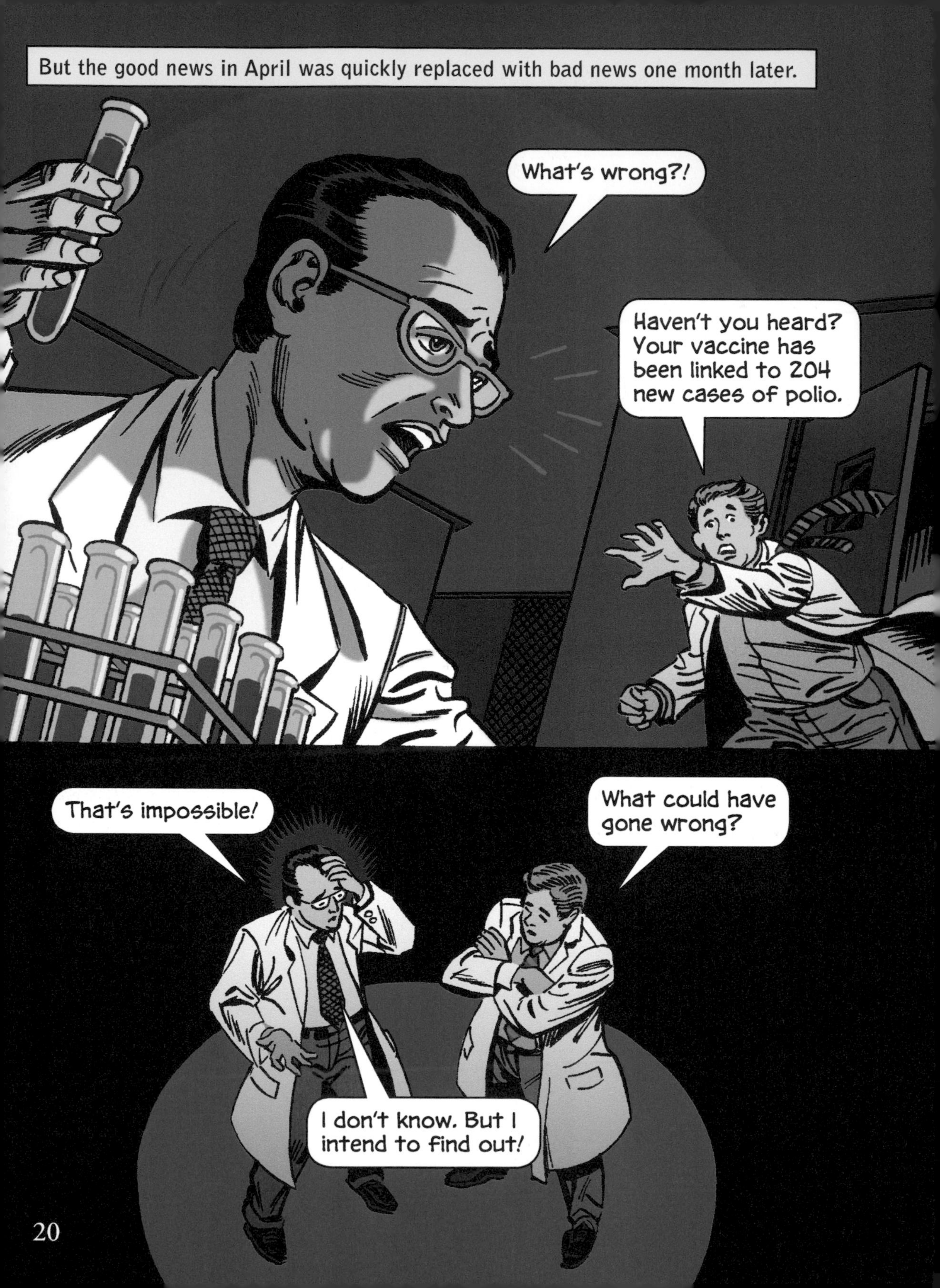
But the good news in April was quickly replaced with bad news one month later.
What's wrong?!
Haven't you heard? Your vaccine has been linked to 204 new cases of polio.
That's impossible!
What could have gone wrong?
I don't know. But I intend to find out!

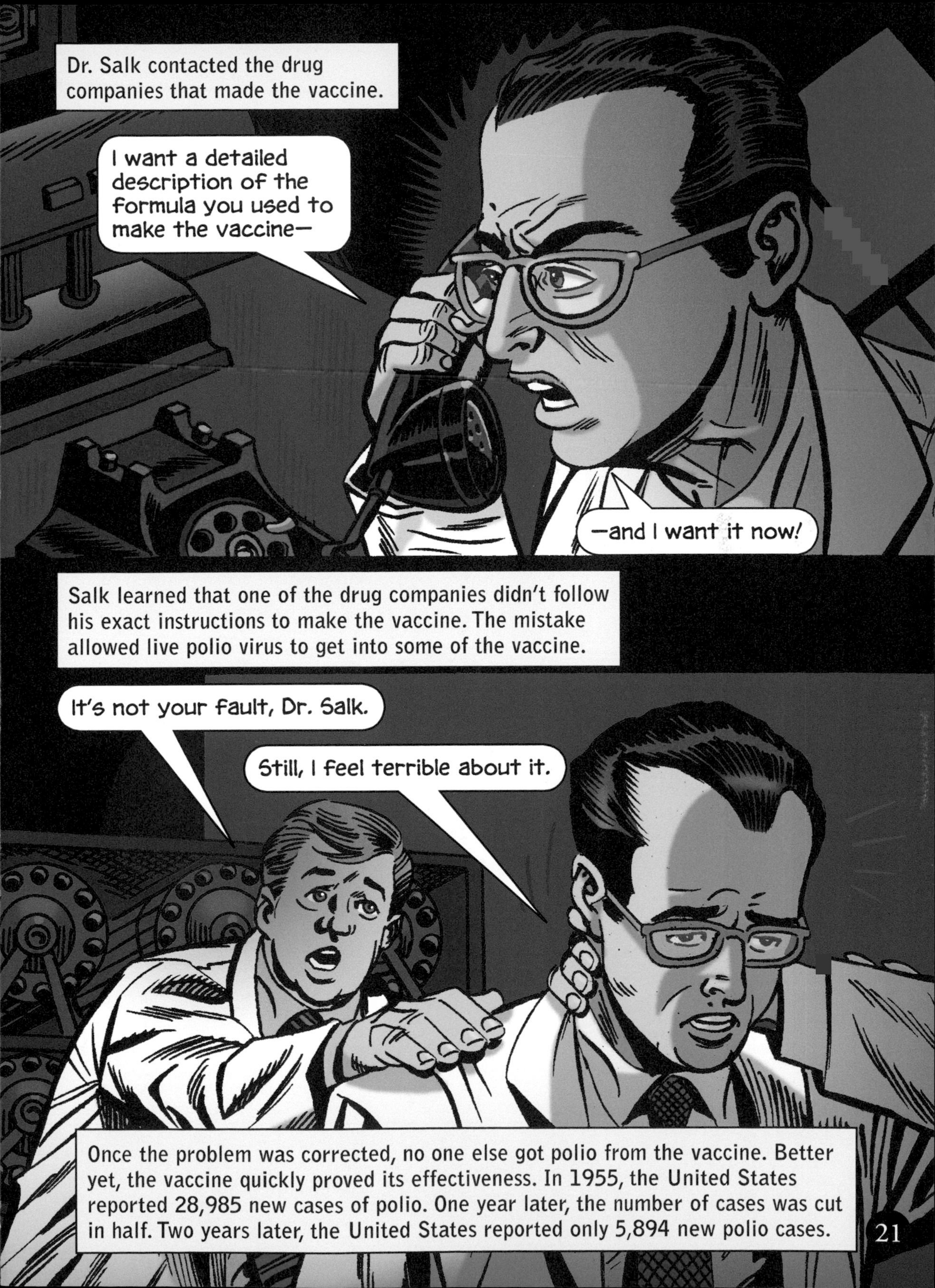
Dr. Salk contacted the drug companies that made the vaccine.
I want a detailed description of the formula you used to make the vaccine—
—and I want it now!
Salk learned that one of the drug companies didn't follow his exact instructions to make the vaccine. The mistake allowed live polio virus to get into some of the vaccine.
It's not your fault, Dr. Salk.
Still, I feel terrible about it.
Once the problem was corrected, no one else got polio from the vaccine. Better yet, the vaccine quickly proved its effectiveness. In 1955, the United States reported 28,985 new cases of polio. One year later, the number of cases was cut in half. Two years later, the United States reported only 5,894 new polio cases.

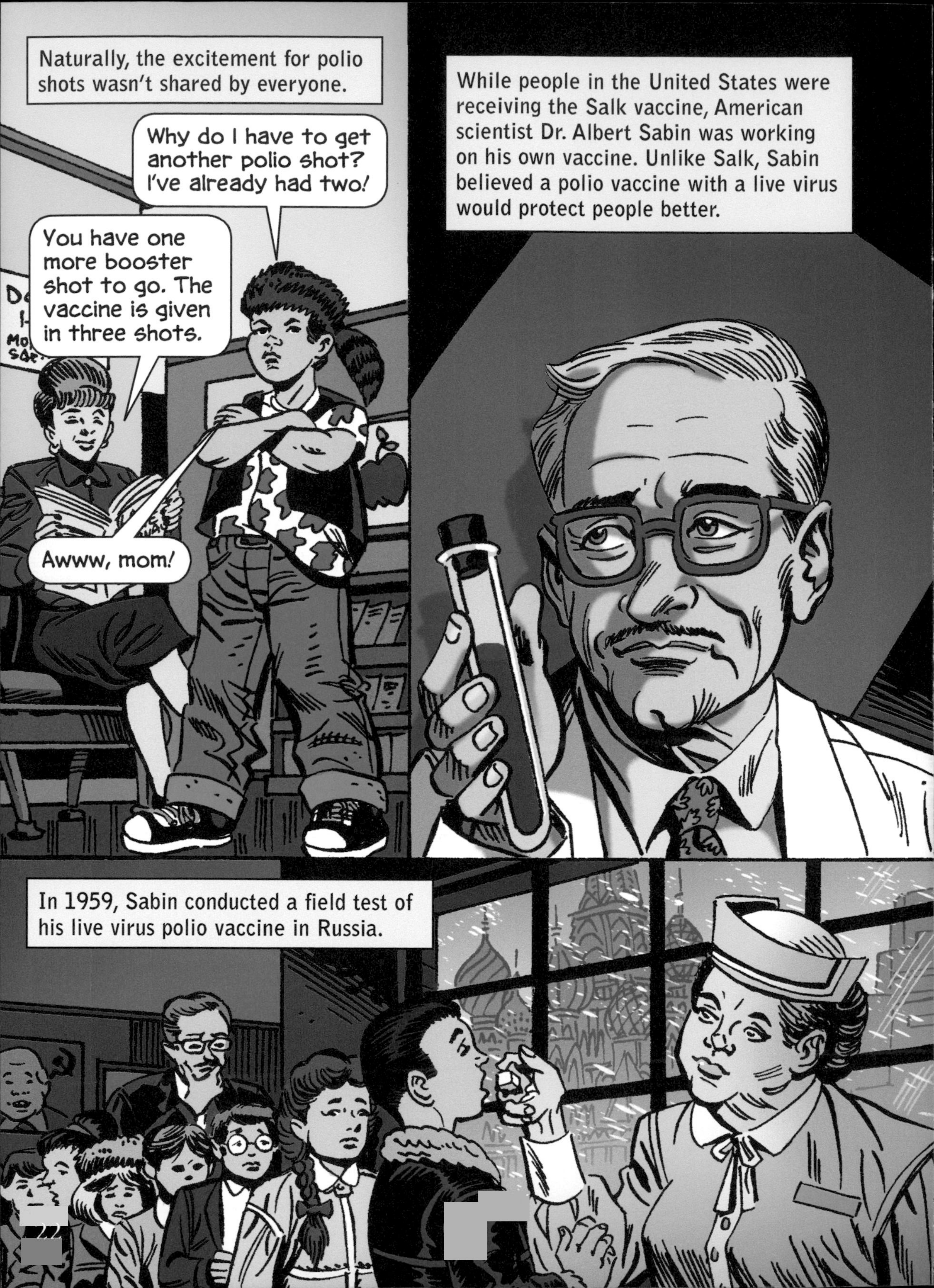
Naturally, the excitement for polio shots wasn't shared by everyone.
Why do I have to get another polio shot? I've already had two!
You have one more booster shot to go. The vaccine is given in three shots.
Awww, mom!
While people in the United States were receiving the Salk vaccine, American scientist Dr. Albert Sabin was working on his own vaccine. Unlike Salk, Sabin believed a polio vaccine with a live virus would protect people better.
In 1959, Sabin conducted a field test of his live virus polio vaccine in Russia.

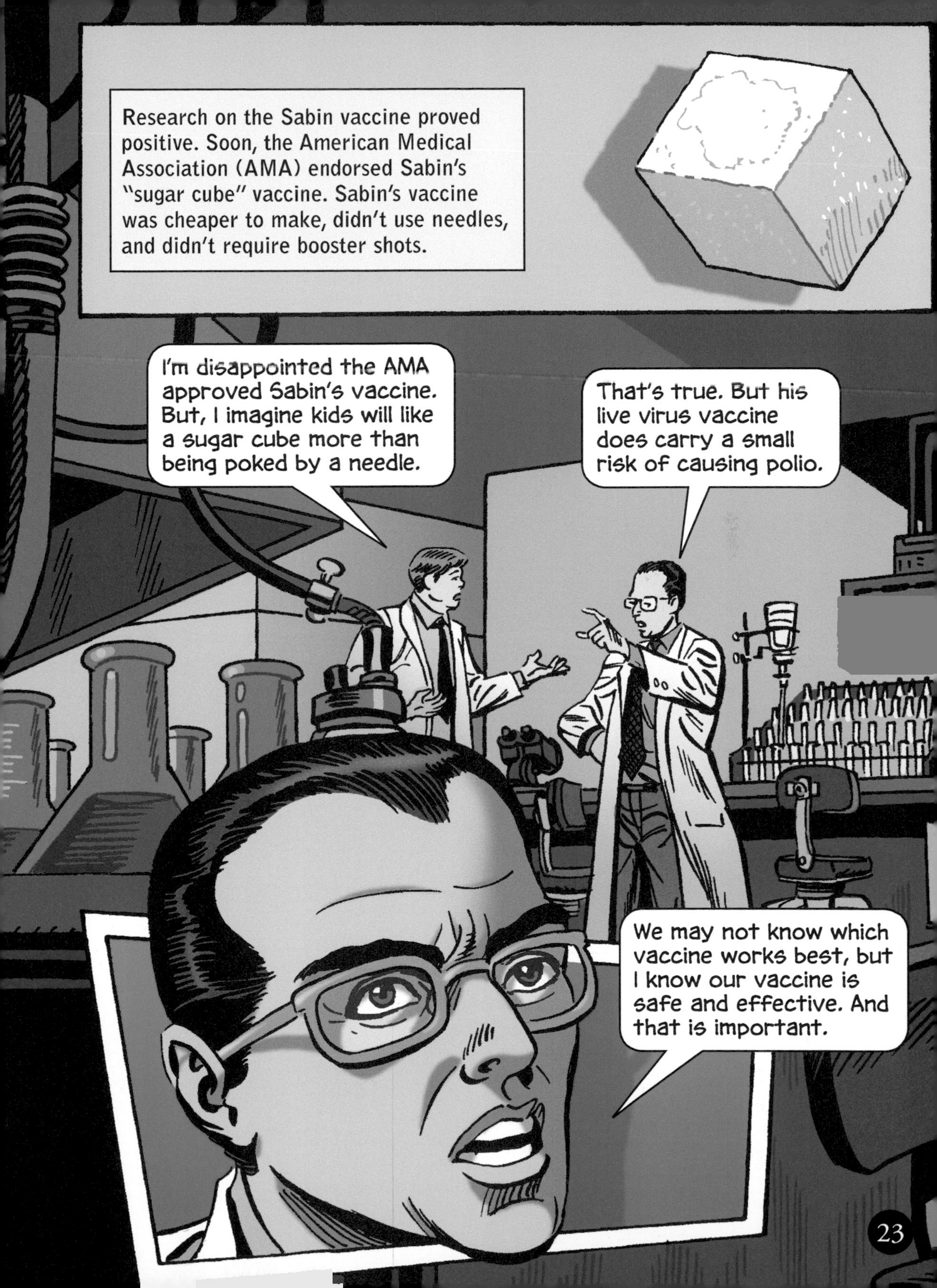
Research on the Sabin vaccine proved positive. Soon, the American Medical Association (AMA) endorsed Sabin's "sugar cube" vaccine. Sabin's vaccine was cheaper to make, didn't use needles, and didn't require booster shots.
I'm disappointed the AMA approved Sabin's vaccine. But, I imagine kids will like a sugar cube more than being poked by a needle.
That's true. But his live virus vaccine does carry a small risk of causing polio.
We may not know which vaccine works best, but I know our vaccine is safe and effective. And that is important.

Chapter 4
A Safer World

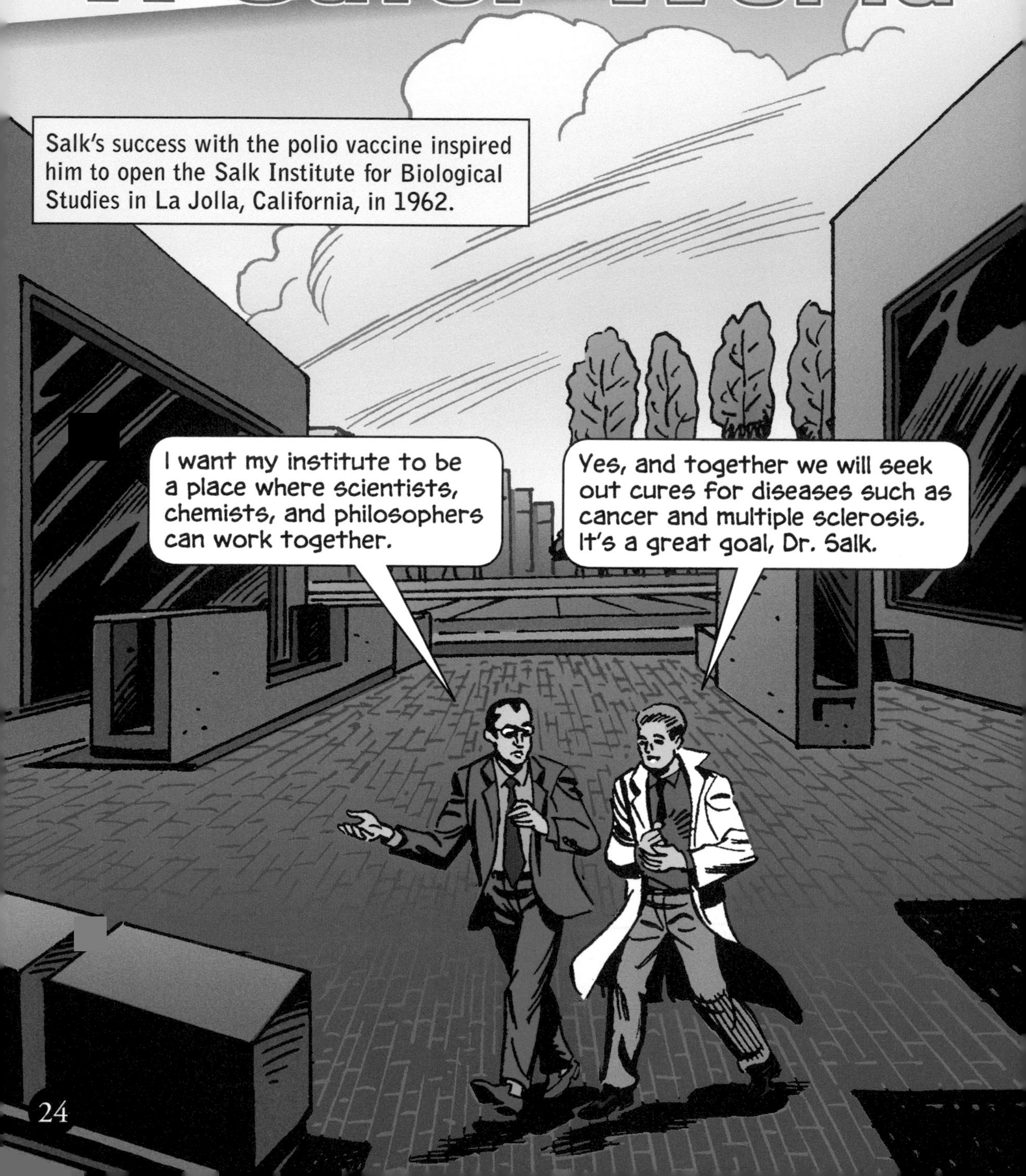

Salk's success with the polio vaccine inspired him to open the Salk Institute for Biological Studies in La Jolla, California, in 1962.
I want my institute to be a place where scientists, chemists, and philosophers can work together.
Yes, and together we will seek out cures for diseases such as cancer and multiple sclerosis. It's a great goal, Dr. Salk.

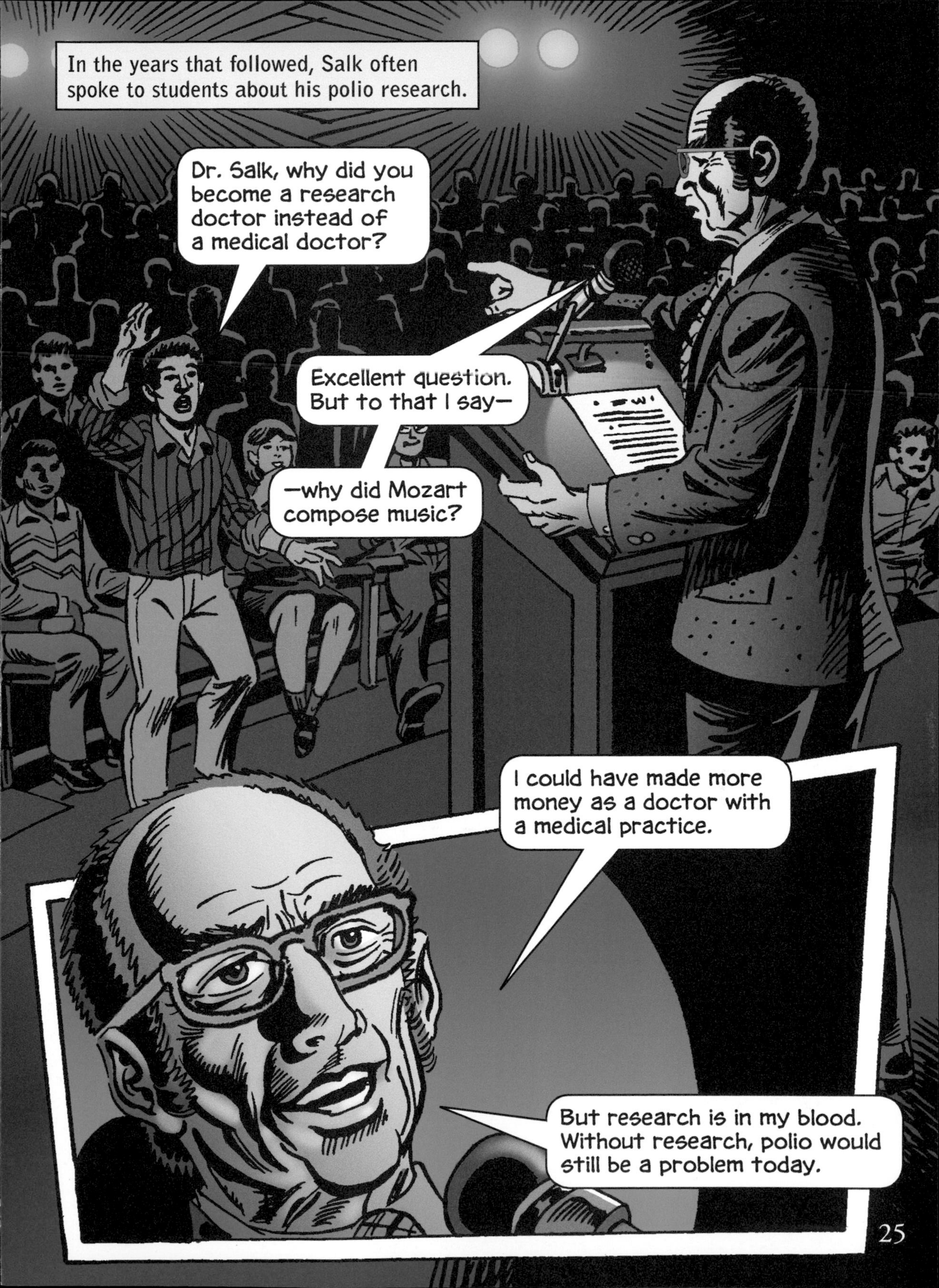
In the years that followed, Salk often spoke to students about his polio research.
Dr. Salk, why did you become a research doctor instead of a medical doctor?
Excellent question. But to that I say—
—why did Mozart compose music?
I could have made more money as a doctor with a medical practice.
But research is in my blood. Without research, polio would still be a problem today.

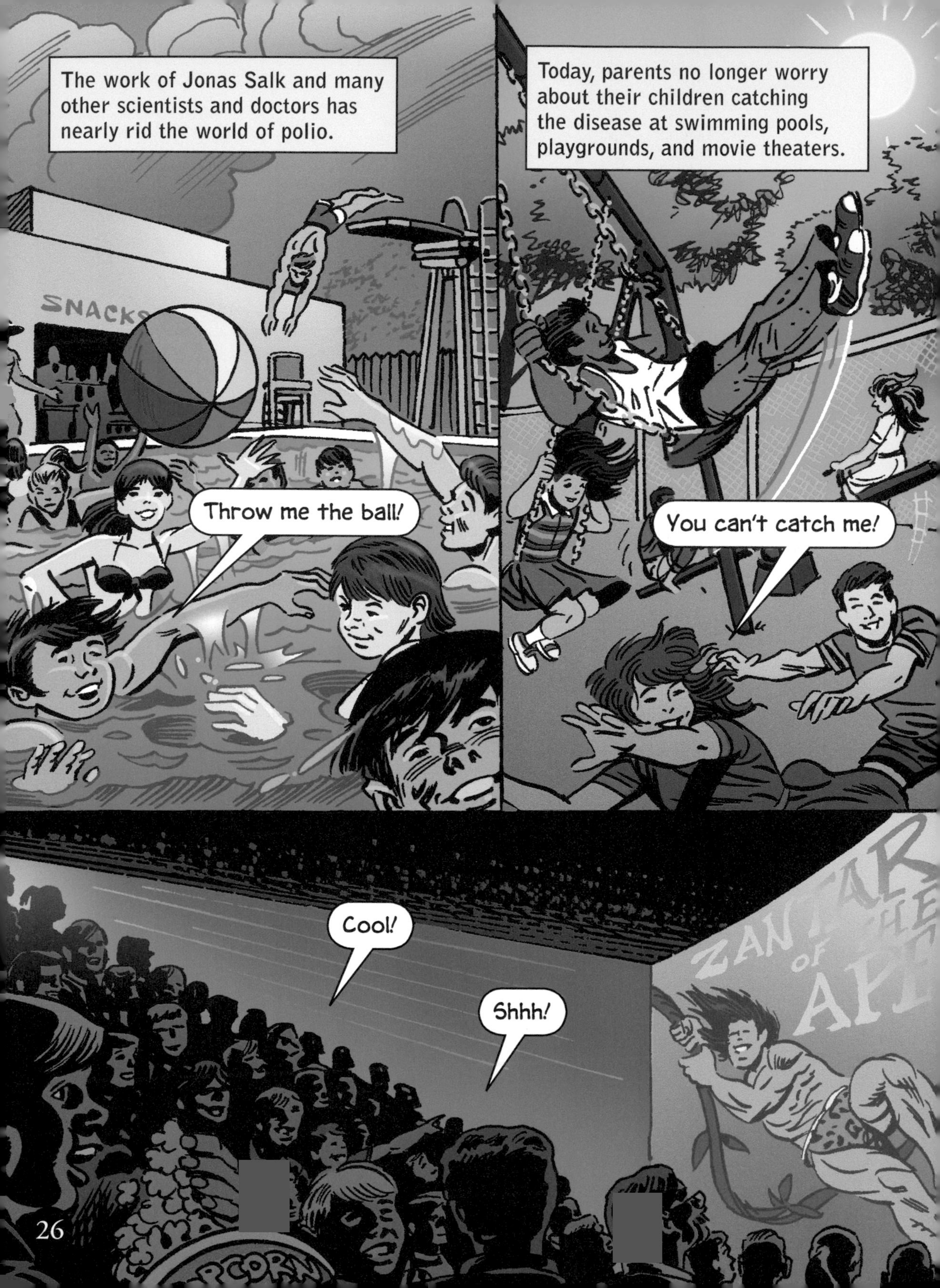
The work of Jonas Salk and many other scientists and doctors has nearly rid the world of polio.
Throw me the ball!
Today, parents no longer worry about their children catching the disease at swimming pools, playgrounds, and movie theaters.
You can't catch me!
Cool!
Shhh!

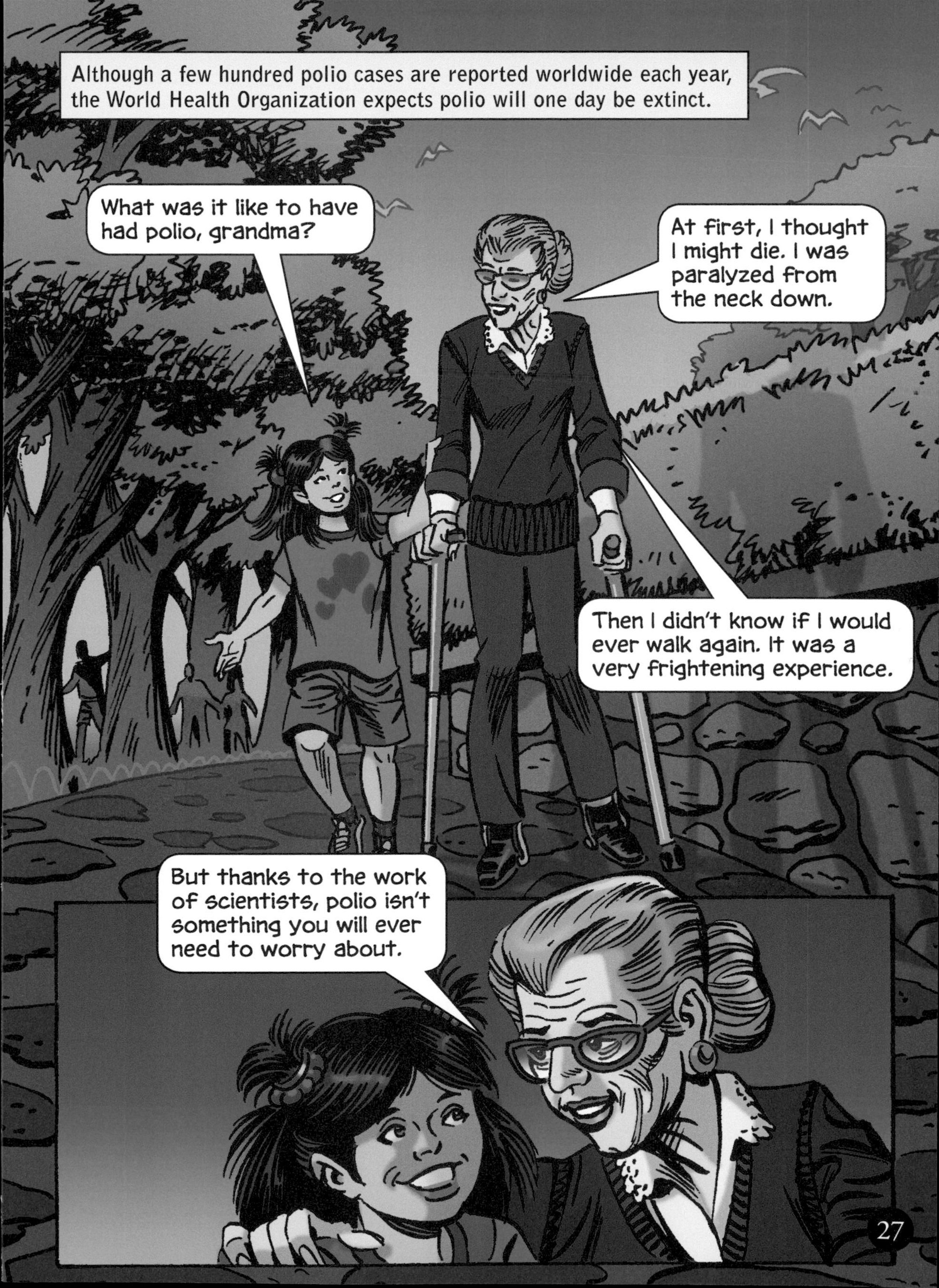
Although a few hundred polio cases are reported worldwide each year, the World Health Organization expects polio will one day be extinct.
What was it like to have had polio, grandma?
At first, I thought I might die. I was paralyzed from the neck down.
Then I didn't know if I would ever walk again. It was a very frightening experience.
But thanks to the work of scientists, polio isn't something you will ever need to worry about.

More about

Jonas Salk and the Polio Vaccine

Jonas Salk was born October 28, 1914, in New York City. His parents were Russian-Jewish immigrants. Although they couldn't afford to send him to college, Salk won scholarships to pay for his education. He graduated from New York University medical school in 1939.

In 1916, when Salk was just a toddler, the worst polio epidemic in history hit the United States. That year 6,000 people were killed by the disease. Another 27,000 people were left paralyzed.

About 1,830,000 children participated in Salk's 1954 field study. But not all of these children received the vaccine. Some children were given a shot made of sugar water and others received no shot at all. These children were part of the control group. The control group allowed researchers to compare polio infection rates between children who got the vaccine and those who didn't.

In the final stages of his polio research, Salk trusted his vaccine so much that he gave it to himself, his wife, and his children.

Polio wasn't a problem in just the United States in the early-1900s. Many other countries were also suffering large polio epidemics. By 1959, more than 90 countries were using Salk's vaccine to fight polio.

By 1962, Albert Sabin's polio vaccine replaced Salk's vaccine in the United States. Although many scientists believed Sabin's live virus vaccine was more effective, it caused about eight cases of polio each year. In 2000, the United States went back to using the Salk vaccine because a killed virus vaccine is safer.

Sabin and Salk disagreed about whether a killed virus or a live virus vaccine was more effective. Their debate caused them to become bitter rivals. Sabin once went so far as to say, "Salk was strictly a kitchen chemist. He never had an original idea in his life."

Jonas Salk died on June 23, 1995. After his death, other researchers carried on his work to fight deadly diseases at the Salk Institute.

GLOSSARY

antibodies (AN-ti-bahd-eez)—proteins made by the body that weaken or destroy invading bacteria, viruses, and poisons

immune system (i-MYOON SISS-tuhm)—part of the body that protects it from diseases by producing antibodies

paralyzed (PAIR-uh-lized)—unable to move or feel

patent (PAT-uhnt)—a legal document that gives an inventor the right to make, use, or sell an invention for a set period of years

vaccine (vak-SEEN)—dead or weakened germs injected into a person or animal to help fight disease

virus (VYE-ruhss)—a tiny particle that infects living things and causes diseases

INTERNET SITES

FactHound offers a safe, fun way to find Internet sites related to this book. All of the sites on FactHound have been researched by our staff.

Here's how:
1. Visit *www.facthound.com*
2. Choose your grade level.
3. Type in this book ID **0736864830** for age-appropriate sites. You may also browse subjects by clicking on letters, or by clicking on pictures and words.
4. Click on the **Fetch It** button.

FactHound will fetch the best sites for you!

READ MORE

Bankston, John. *Jonas Salk and the Polio Vaccine.*
Unlocking the Secrets of Science. Bear, Del.: Mitchell
Lane, 2002.

Durrett, Deanne. *Jonas Salk.* Inventors and Creators.
Detroit: Kidhaven Press, 2002.

Hecht, Alan. *Polio.* Deadly Diseases and Epidemics.
Philadelphia: Chelsea House, 2003.

McPherson, Stephanie Sammartino. *Jonas Salk: Conquering
Polio.* A Lerner Biography. Minneapolis: Lerner, 2002.

Parks, Peggy J. *Jonas Salk: Polio Vaccine Pioneer.* Giants
of Science. San Diego: Blackbirch Press, 2004.

BIBLIOGRAPHY

Carter, Richard. *Breakthrough: The Saga of Jonas Salk.*
New York: Trident Press, 1966.

Kluger, Jeffrey. *Splendid Solution: Jonas Salk and the
Conquest of Polio.* New York: G. P. Putnam's Sons, 2004.

Oshinsky, David. *Polio: An American Story.* New York:
Oxford University Press, 2005.

Williams, Greer. *Virus Hunters.* New York: Knopf, 1959.

INDEX